THE
GRANDPARENTING
GUIDE
FOR THE
ROCK-N-ROLL
GENERATION

PAT BURNS

New York

Grandparents Rock : The Grandparenting Guide for the Rock-n-Roll Generation

ISBN: 978-1-60037-303-9

Published by:

Morgan James Publishing, LLC
1225 Franklin Ave. Ste 325
Garden City, NY 11530-1693
Toll Free 800-485-4943
www.MorganJamesPublishing.com

Cover design:
Dunn+Associates   www.dunn-design.com

Interior and back cover design:
Chaz DeSimone   www.chazdesimone.com

Photographs of the author:
Maria Rangel   www.mariaphotography.com

To my grandchildren

DYLAN ROBERT VANDENBERG
and

SKYE ELIZABETH SMITH

for gifting me with countless hours of joy

AND

To my grandmother

MAGDALENA (LENKA) FABJANIĆ RAJS

for her gifts of strength, character,
quirkiness and unconditional love

♥

CONTENTS

Grandparents *ROCK*

viii

FOREWORD
by **MARK VICTOR HANSEN**

I'm not sure if "The Times They Are a-Changin" is a rock and roll song, but the famous anthem by Bob Dylan—by the way, he's a grandparent!—definitely captured the sprit of his generation. Actually, "The Times Are a-Changin" could easily be the subtitle of the book you now hold in your hands, because as you may already know, being a grandparent can rock your world. Well, I can assure you that Pat Burns' *Grandparents Rock* will rock your soul. It certainly did rock mine.

These are the real stories of flesh and blood human beings, and they're also the portrait of an amazing demographic transformation. Seventy-five million Americans are going to pass the age of 60 during the first two decades of the twenty-first century. In the past, people in this age group were ready for retirement, which meant golf, fishing, or just sitting on the back porch. But now age is becoming irrelevant as a determining factor of what we can do. More importantly, age is irrelevant in terms of what we *want* to do. Our years are no longer a valid measure of our capabilities, our interests, or even our physical health. Regardless of what the calendar says, our own intentions and desires will determine what we do from now on.

As Pat's book makes splendidly clear, what the baby boomers want to do in terms of grandparenting is....well, it's a *lot!* "Different Strokes for Different

Folks" is definitely the order of the day, but everybody you'll meet in these pages hopes to play a major, positive role in the lives of their grandchildren. To some extent they want this because they know an extended family is a good child-rearing environment, but mostly they want to be involved because it's so much fun. The folks in these pages just love this new stage in their lives. Regardless of where they are, what color they are, how much money they have, or even what kind of music they like, they totally enjoy grandparenting. If you have grandchildren, I know you'll connect with what they're talking about. Even if you aren't a grandparent, seeing this much joy on the page is a great experience. You might want to run out and change a diaper!

But beyond the sheer exuberance of *Grandparents Rock*, there is also an important message. As society has changed, grandparents have a much more dynamic role than was true a few decades in the past. Today there are two parent families, one-parent families, adoptive families, single sex two parent families, and all the other possible combinations. We no longer live in the Hallmark card image of Mom-Dad-kids type family. But in my opinion one thing is a constant: parents shouldn't make this journey alone, because they need all the help they can get. Fortunately, as the demands of raising kids have grown more complex, this amazing number of grandparents has suddenly arrived just yearning to lend a hand. Weird! And great!

Pat has found a brilliant way of expressing all this through the cross-generational medium of rock and roll. Who would ever have thought that Beatles songs would come to be known as kids' music? But we never thought either that "When I'm Sixty-four" would be just around the corner. It's amazing, it's complicated, it's new, it's timeless, it's just a tiny bit scary, but the bottom line is: "it's all good."

No matter where you are in the demographic profile, I know you'll love *Grandparents Rock*. Rock on!

INTRODUCTION

Becoming a grandparent is always an amazing experience, but as the rock-n-roll generation enters this new phase of life, there's really something different going on. These are people—and I definitely include myself among them—who never really expected to age. From the beginning, we members of the baby boom generation were told (and we told ourselves) that we were outside the norm in every way. And we believed it. Most of us would have agreed with the author William Saroyan, who late in life remarked, "I always knew people got old. But I thought an exception would be made in my case."

Now that the first baby boomers are entering their 60s, the rest of the world may see this as somewhat of a comeuppance. But I beg to differ. I still don't believe I'm old or that I'm going to get old. Whatever the calendar might say, I still don't plan on moving into a conventional "senior citizen's" lifestyle. In my work, in my play, in the way I dress, in the food I eat, in the music I listen to and certainly in the way I interact with my grandchildren, I have no intention of being either tired or retired. Nor, as you'll see, do the many contributors to this book. As the song says, "Rock-n-roll is here to stay"—so bring it on!

In these pages you'll see the many different styles and feelings that "rock-n-roll grandparenting" can express. Classic rock-n-roll songs serve as chapter titles, reflecting the feelings and memories of the contributors whose interviews are the essence of this book. I hope reminiscing about these songs will take you back over the rollercoaster ride of your earlier years—both the happy times and the heartbreaks. Perhaps your recollections will help you, as they have me, to fully enjoy this new phase of your life, which is all about pure love. That pure love awaits us regardless of our age, our financial circumstances or any health challenges we may be facing.

Like the colors of a rainbow, there are literally dozens of grandparenting configurations in today's world: adopted grandchildren, grandchildren from different sets of parents, single-parented grandchildren, grandchildren from all races—it's all happening right now. But within all these different family configurations, there is one constant theme and one consistent message: We all love being grandparents. It's a completely joyful, transformational part of life.

That is one aspect that really sets grandparenting apart from everything else. Ever heard the expression "It's all good"? Well, grandparenting really is "all good." Nobody wants their money back, ever.

I say this from experience. I wouldn't be writing a book for grandparents if I were not a grandparent myself. My daughter, Jennifer, has blessed me with wonderful grandchildren—whom you'll meet in these pages. The word "blessed" is chosen carefully. For me, the birth of a grandchild really is a sacred and magical event . . .

At 2:53 a.m., I arrived at the Tucson birth center to welcome my precious new granddaughter, just minutes after her entry into our family. Surrounded by soft lights and still damp from her water birth, baby Skye captured all our hearts without even making a sound. My daughter, Jennifer, had done everything in her power to make Skye's birthing experience quiet, peaceful and full of love. Understandably, Jennifer had high expectations. As a certified nurse midwife, she prepared for this birth as if it were the most significant test of her life—like taking the bar exam a hundred times over. This birth had to be natural and as peaceful as possible. Though it meant a two-hour car trip (in hard labor) to the birth center in Tucson, Jennifer's wish came true. She and the baby "kept it together" long enough to reach the environment Jennifer had envisioned. I now had my second grandchild.

More than *ever*, I recognize and appreciate all the inspired coincidences—the *synchronicities*—that life has to offer. The birth of Skye has to be at the top of my synchronicity list. Between September 2004 and October 2005, I traveled to San Diego, Tahiti, Salt Lake City, Orlando, Dallas, Chicago, New York, Maui, Philadelphia, Washington DC, Banff, Belize and Honduras —and climbed Mount Whitney! With all that traveling, what were the chances I would end up in the same state, and even in the same city, on the exact day of my granddaughter's birth—even though the predicted date of birth was three weeks later? I don't believe even the Vegas odds makers would have taken a bet on that one!

But as it happened, in the months before Skye's birth I was making plans to host an educational event in Sedona, Arizona, for a group of 100 business leaders known as The Inner Circle. I would be joined there by my long-time clients Mark Victor Hansen and Robert Allen. While planning the Sedona trip, I learned, quite by accident, that His Holiness the Dalai Lama would be giving a presentation in Tucson, Arizona. Just one day before the tickets were to be sold, I called the convention center and managed to prepurchase 100 seats. The pieces of the puzzle were beginning to come together, but this was only the beginning. Through some friends who were in charge of the pre-events—the Friends of Tibet luncheon and the Interfaith Council meeting—I was able to arrange for Mark, Bob and myself to be VIP guests at a special by-invitation-only luncheon featuring the Dalai Lama. All this was arranged months before my daughter's due date, let alone the day on which Skye was actually born.

The luncheon banquet room was set for 400 guests. Bob, Mark and I were seated at the center table directly in front of the head table. The Dalai Lama sat to the left and directly in front of me. Security guards stood close to him and would gently redirect anyone who approached. While the guests at each table waited for lunch to be served, I pulled out a small piece of yellow paper and wrote down my intention for this experience of being with the Dalai Lama: "My granddaughter was born today. Would you please give her your blessing?"

As I watched His Holiness listening attentively to the person seated beside him, I suddenly realized that he and I were looking directly at each other. I smiled and, completely without thinking, gave him a tiny childish wave, as you would when playing with a baby. Immediately, he stopped his conversation and mirrored my playful gesture back to me. In response, I clasped my hands in a prayer position, held them at my forehead and gave a more respectful, bowed acknowledgment. As before, he returned the same.

There we were smiling at each other, and for a moment, the guards who were once stopping people from approaching His Holiness were no longer there. Seeing the opportunity, I rose from my chair, gently passed him my slip of paper and returned to my seat.

I watched as he carefully opened the paper and read my note. He showed it to the man sitting beside him, who read my special prayer request to His Holiness, asking for his blessing. The Dalai Lama looked at me, smiled and nodded his head with a yes. I watched at that very moment as my granddaughter, just barely 10 hours old, received from His Holiness a prayer and his blessing. Skye Elizabeth Smith's birth will be blessed always.

This is one of my own grandparenting stories, and to me it is indeed very special. But it's no more remarkable than many you've experienced yourself or that you will read here. In their different ways, they all express the amazing experience of being a grandparent from the rock-n-roll generation. I wrote *Grandparents Rock* to meet the changing needs of my generation. I wanted the book to be a fast, fun and easy read. The messages you'll read here were contributed from dozens of grandparents interviewed for this book. Some excerpts are very short; some are much longer. Some are carefully composed and elegantly expressed. Others are like a casual conversation with a person who happens to be seated beside you on a plane trip. Undoubtedly, some of them will be more in sync with your own feelings than others. My hope is that at least one of them—and perhaps many of them—will be exactly what you need to hear at the exact moment you are reading it.

Being with Skye and with my grandson, Dylan, has brought me more joy than I ever imagined possible.

It's the freedom to love completely and to embrace and enjoy this special time. That's my wish for you and for everyone who reads this book.

At the end of each section and at the back of this book, you'll find some blank pages where you can add your own thoughts and feelings. I hope what you read here will inspire you to jot down any activities, stories, family traditions or other ideas you've used for creating strong bonds with your grandchildren. Feel free to ask your friends to share their ideas too. And I'd love to hear your stories and experiences. You can reach me through my website, www.grand-parentsrock.com. I would like to mention also that a portion of the proceeds from this book will be used to support literacy, through Timeless Learning Inc., a nonprofit corporation that produces the Orange County Children's Book Festival. To learn more or to make a donation, please visit www.kidsbookfestival.com.

Grandparents *ROCK*

xx

Grandparents
ROCK

45
RP

SHAKE, RATTLE AND ROLL

Life is what we make it.

Always has been, always will be.

Grandma Moses

CHAPTER 1

SHAKE RATTLE AND ROLL

"Shake, Rattle and Roll" is the perfect song for this first chapter, which is all about the reactions of the rock-n-roll generation to becoming grandparents. The lyrics "Get out in that kitchen and rattle those pots and pans" will surely resonate with new grandparents, especially if they're helping the new parents with housework or babysitting. What song title could express the first-time grandparenting experience better than "Shake, Rattle and Roll"? The realization, joyful though it is, that you're no longer the second-youngest generation in your family can be earth shaking and soul stirring. It might rattle you for a moment. But by learning to roll with the shifting tide, you will start to rock. You will rock 'n' roll as never before!

It may take a while to get there, however. Becoming a grandparent sets off a variety of emotions in different people. My mother, for instance, seemed not at all pleased when I announced I was pregnant; she went into complete denial, as if she could somehow make it all disappear. I've often wondered why she responded this way. She was 55, about the average age to begin having grandchildren. Why didn't she approach this rite of passage with the same zest she brought to other aspects of her life? Perhaps her vanity had something to do with it. She was a beautiful woman, looking younger than her years, with a successful career in real estate, and active in arts and service groups. But in some ways she was quite uncertain about herself. How she saw herself was strongly influenced by how she believed others saw her. If she thought that becoming a grandparent made her look older to other people, then she also looked older to herself.

I remember being five months pregnant and just beginning to show. My mother and I were out shopping in a department store—one of our favorite activities—and met one of her "society ladies." While they were chatting about their next concert or party, I noticed my mother moving in front of my body to hide my "baby stomach." This was the first of several times I recognized the shame my mother seemed to be feeling. Sometimes she displayed outright anger. When she could no longer simply move in front of me to conceal my showing, she would declare that I was much too young to begin a family. But if there was an age issue here, it certainly was more about her age than mine.

Right then I made a promise to myself: When the time came, I would embrace this passage differently. When it was my turn to become a grandparent, I would be proud! I would brag about it to everyone! I would be the perfect mother of a pregnant daughter!

Then God threw me a curveball. I became a grandmother at 43—a little younger than the norm, a lot younger than my mom had been. There was a whole lot of shakin' goin' on: it was the launch of a roller-coaster experience.

My smart, talented and altogether dazzling daughter was in her senior year of high school. When Jennifer said, "I have some news, Mom," my first thought was it was about her choice of a college. She was an honors student in the top 5 percent of her class, and she had applied to UC Santa Cruz, UCLA and UC Berkeley. I was sure she'd have her pick.

The truth is that I was definitely shaken by what she said that day. I simply had to roll with her choice to have her baby. It seems incredible to me now, but at first it seemed to me like a decision she would regret. Yet it has been the most wonderful blessing and gift for us all.

Just 15 days before the Christmas that followed, my love affair with my grandson began. I was actually in the delivery room with Jennifer to welcome Dylan. Watching my daughter bring a new life into the world—and seeing in Dylan's face an immediate reflection of my entire heritage—was truly the moment of a lifetime!

The rockin' grandparents you'll meet in this chapter have all experienced that same gift of astonishing love, but they've all arrived there along different paths. For some, this amazing event happened just as they had always hoped it would. Others found the transition to becoming a grandparent happening in more unexpected ways. But all that is secondary to the totally glorious, hugely exciting, absolutely wonderful experience that awaits every grandparent. However it is delivered to you, this is a gift that you will always treasure.

6

When I first learned I was going to be a grandmother, I was struck. I was shaken. I wasn't ready for it. It took some getting used to. I felt like my son was very young, and the woman he was involved with was very much older than he was. I was feeling very at odds with a lot of things. It was shake, rattle and roll, for sure!

I remember my husband coming home and saying, "I've got something to tell you." The way he said it, it sounded so serious; for some reason I thought he was going to leave me. I put my head down and said, "You're leaving already?" We had only been married three years. Then he said, "You're going to be a grandmother."

We decided we had to go for a walk, so we walked around the park. It was hard. That's how I felt about it at first. Mostly, it was concern about my son and the woman. It wasn't like they were two people who had gotten married and had been wanting to have children. I didn't even know that my son and this woman were in that kind of relationship. It wasn't about the end of my youth or anything like that; it had nothing to do with "I'm not ready to be old." I just didn't know what to do or say.

But I've learned it's actually a good thing when you don't know what to do, because then fresh things happen in you and new things grow. You learn how to love. You learn to have compassion. You learn acceptance. You learn forgiveness. You learn to listen. You learn to shut up. You have to learn those things, and you have to change in order to get yourself together.

I had to change because the person who was carrying my granddaughter was a member of the choir I direct. She was in my second-soprano section and loved the choir. She was always at rehearsal, and she loved me, too.

I had never considered myself a minister of my faith until then, but becoming a grandmother and dealing with these emotions challenged me to grow. I had to help the choir forgive, because there were a lot of negative feelings and opinions flying around about this woman. People had known my son for a long time. I had to help them heal; and at the same time, I relied on my daughter to help me with my own healing. She said, "Hey, we can all have our opinions. But this woman is carrying my little niece, and your granddaughter, so we have to just get over it." You see, my son's girlfriend is a white girl, and my son is black. I'm with both black and white people all the time, and I've never had any problems interacting with anyone until the girl who comes home to my family is a white girl. It was like, "Whoa, where did these feelings come from?"

My granddaughter's name is Jada. She looks just like me and she's musical like me. She dances, she loves music, she knows songs. I tell everybody that she didn't come from her mother or her daddy—she came from me! She's going to be my new choir director when I step down from my position someday.

RICKIE B.B.
Los Angeles, California

When I learned I was going to become a grandparent, I remembered back to the time I found out about my own pregnancy—when I was pregnant with Casey. My husband and I had been married seven years, and we'd tried to become pregnant. Sadly, it hadn't worked out for us. We had lost a baby about five months into my pregnancy. It was a terrible miscarriage that almost took me with it. I was in the hospital for a week and was told by the doctors that I would probably never get pregnant again. I remember how heartbroken we were to have lost our first baby and then how difficult it was to get pregnant after that.

When I found out I was pregnant again, with Casey, we went out and celebrated with all our friends. I remember that joy I felt when I realized that I was preg-

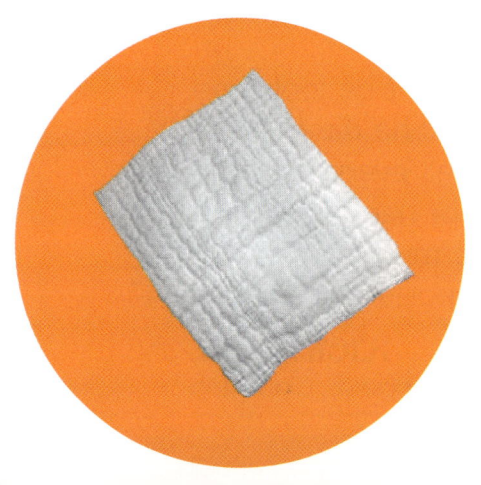

then

Diapers were just large squares of soft cloth. They're still used today... for polishing cars.

nant again; I had another chance! Years later, when I heard that our son was going to be a father, it was like a déjà vu feeling, and I thought, "Oh, Casey, you have so much ahead of you. Wait until you experience this. It will change your life forever."

My first impression was that I was so happy for him. I knew what lay ahead and how it had transformed our lives when we'd found out we were expecting. And then I realized, "Oh my gosh, I'm going to be a grandmother? I'm way too young to be a grandmother!" I said to him, "Okay, we have one rule here: Nobody calls me Grandma."

He laughed and said, "You can have the baby call you whatever you want."

My mother was 19 when she gave birth to me, and her mother was 21 when she gave birth to her. My grandmother was 40 when I was born—we have a family history of young grandmothers. My grandmother refused to be called Grandma or Granny or anything like that. She was living in the Philippines when I was born, so she told my mother to call her Nana. Now I'm Nonny and my husband is Poppy.

Have my thoughts or feelings changed since I first learned that I would be a grandparent? Well, yes, and it has been an exciting process for me. My daughter-in-law and I are very close; she's not very close with her own biological mother. I not only had the privilege of having a daughter all of a sudden—and the feeling seems to be very mutual—but I also had the privilege of having a mom's role with a pregnant daughter. The entire pregnancy was an enriching experience for us.

JEANNE C.
Los Vegas, Nevada

 have only one son and only one granddaughter, so perhaps this is my only chance in this lifetime to experience being a grandparent. When my son, Ryan, and my daughter-in-law, Christy, telephoned me in Quito, Ecuador, where I was living at the time, to tell me they were expecting, I began that series of dream weaving that I'm sure all potential grandmothers do.

Right from the start we were expecting a girl, and I was thrilled. A granddaughter! Could I be this lucky? The news alone painted my world pink! Love was in the air. I was in love with my granddaughter from the moment she appeared as a heartbeat in an ultrasound scan.

With my being a writer, you can imagine what a great future I envisioned for my granddaughter and me, but for the most part I was asking no more than what all grandparents desire. I thought of holidays with the family around the table, the perfectly golden brown turkey being carved proudly by my son, the rolls that this particular time I managed not to burn, and the cake that miraculously did not fall. I envisioned taking my granddaughter to Paris, where we would visit the Louvre and then the street artists of the Left Bank so she could know that talent and genius do not necessarily go hand in hand with fame or immortality. I wanted to be with her on Halloween and at Easter Morning services. I would spoon-feed her doses of wisdom I have learned from some serious hard knocks of life. I would show her that having fun was more important than worrying, and I would hug her every chance I had. I would give her as much love as I had given my son all his life, but I would do it with a Barbie doll in hand!

I would make her a dollhouse with my own hands and pray she cherished it; but if she broke it, she would realize it was only a toy. I would let her roll on the floor with all eight of my Golden Retriever puppies so she would know the smell of puppy breath and the touch of a puppy's love in her heart. I would be her best friend and spoil her rotten. And we would be together forever.

When Caylin was born, the rest of the family and I remained in the hospital waiting room until two in the morning, when the doctor blessedly allowed us to see Christy and Ryan and to hold Caylin. My first words to her were "I love you," and my first promise was "Someday I will be the first person to take you to Paris."

n o w

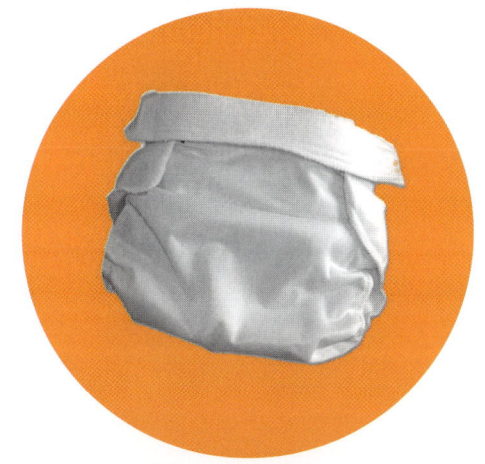

Cloth diapers are making a comeback, replacing plastic. But today they're pre-folded, fitted and disposable.

All the other promises and dreams I had for Caylin I kept inside my head; I managed to make most of them come true over the next five years. For the first year of Caylin's life, distance was a problem in our relationship because I was still flying back and forth from Ecuador. Then life settled down somewhat. I built a house in Houston, and I believed that although I had owned more than a dozen homes in my life, perhaps if I built one from scratch, I would be able to stay there the rest of my life.

I made a room for Caylin in that house, complete with a dollhouse, a table and chairs for her tea parties, plenty of stuffed animals, dolls and games. When she was about three, we began a monthly routine of her coming to visit me for a long sleepover. What began as an overnight slumber party stretched to two days, then three. And of course when she grew up enough, we went on a plane trip together. Just us. No parents. No really big rules. We were gypsies together.

CATHERINE L.
Scottsdale, Arizona

atthew and Rachel are my grandchildren. They're my daughter's kids. I had always wanted to be a grandmother, but unfortunately my daughter was not able to conceive. Both grandchildren are adopted. When Tammy found out that she definitely could not conceive, I said, "Okay, Plan B. There are lots of babies out there waiting for us."

Matthew joined our family when he was just a few hours old. We thought we would have to wait a lot longer for an adoption, but fortunately for us, his was very quick. Tammy got a phone call the night before he was born. He was born in Washington State. She called me and was hysterical on one end, and I was hysterical on the other end—jumping up and down! Immediately Tammy and her husband went up to Washington to meet their new baby.

They had to spend a couple of weeks in Seattle, and I was just dying because I couldn't go along. I saw my grandson for the first time when he was just about two weeks old. And from the minute I put that little boy in my arms, I just couldn't get enough of him. To me, he's the most perfect little guy in the whole world. I just can't tell you my elation. I knew that we'd have our babies one way or another.

Matthew's was a closed adoption, which meant we

didn't know his birth mother. Our second grandchild, Rachel, was an open adoption. I got to meet her birth mother and her family. My daughter and husband arrived where she'd been born within a few hours, and I got there the following morning. Again, it was just wonderful. I took one look at her and I thought, "Oh my God, this is perfect. Life is complete."

LORRAINE T.
Fullerton, California

 have four grand-children. My daughter's twins are 14 months. From my husband's family there's Tommy, who's four. And recently my daughter-in-law gave birth to Jacob. He's almost three months old.

When I first found out I was going to be a grand-parent, my daughter told me that she had a little gift for me. I didn't think much of it because we exchange gifts all the time, you know? I was teasing her on the phone: "Am I gonna look real cute in it?" She said, "Well, I'm not sure. You'll have to see." I went over to her house, and she had a gift bag with a ribbon and some pretty tissue. I looked inside and there was a book: Grandparenting ABC's: A Beginner's Hand-book. I just looked at her for a second, and then I started crying and hugging her. I remember feeling that I was in a dream, because I had wished for this moment for so long.

But when reality set in, I started worrying about everything. It was even worse than when I was preg-nant with my daughter, or right after she was born. It seems like there's so much more to worry about now—so many health issues, even fear about babies getting their shots. I'm just a huge worrywart now!

JANE M.
Azusa, California

ntil I was about five years old, my grandmother and one of my aunts lived with my family. My grandmother was not really so old at that time—probably in her early 60s—but as I remember it, she seemed very old and very different. She was born in Russia, no one was sure exactly when, and she had very long gray hair that she usually wore in braids. She never learned to speak English very well. She used to make mistakes that seemed hilariously funny to me, like calling a knife a comb.

I was 56 when my grandson Matt was born—not so much younger than my grandmother was when I was born, but I'm much more in tune with what's going on than she was able to be. My husband and I were really ready and eager to become grandparents, but we had thought my son and his wife were going to wait another year. It was great news when we found out. Now Matt is six, and his little brother, Jacob, is almost three.

For me, there was one really amazing difference between the birth of my grandchildren and what happened when my own kids were born. The difference was actually very simple: I was fully conscious when attending my grandchildren's births. When I had my kids, the standard procedure was to use general anesthesia. They knocked you out. You woke up, and it was all over. This conscious birth—being awake—was something very new and exciting for me. I was not actually there at the moment of birth, but I was in the next room, and we were able to see the baby very soon. By nature I'm a very practical person, but Matt's birth was very emotional for me, maybe because of how I'd been knocked out when I became a mom. My husband and I were in the labor room at first, then we were in a waiting room, and about an hour later Matt was born. When I saw Matt, I just felt like I would throw myself in front of a bus or a train for him. He was definitely a keeper!

LYNN M.
Chicago, Illinois

 have one grandchild, and his name is Donovan. He's my firstborn's firstborn. I'm also a firstborn, and so was my dad, so that's a family tradition we're enjoying.

Here's how I first learned that I was going to become a grandparent: Our oldest son, Casey, had been going with a girl for about five years, through high school and into young adulthood. We despised her, and she despised us. It was a terrible relationship; and although we tried our best to love her, she was just a difficult person. Fortunately they broke up, and Casey started dating all these beautiful, gorgeous young things and Budweiser girls and models; he himself is a very good-looking young man.

He had his share of lovely girls chasing him around. But he wasn't happy. He kept saying, "You know, I want to find my soul mate." He really wanted to be married. He's just that kind of person. He eventually ended up meeting a young lady through one of the online dating services. She was in New York City, but then he learned she was moving out here to live with her mother. When they met, it was love at first sight—he was totally smitten.

He came home and told us he'd met this beautiful girl named Paula and he wanted us to meet her. He said, "I know this sounds crazy, but I think she's the one." We met her, and she was wonderful in every aspect. They got very serious and decided they were perfect for each other, and they wanted to get married. This was after they had been dating for six months, and they wanted to get married six months

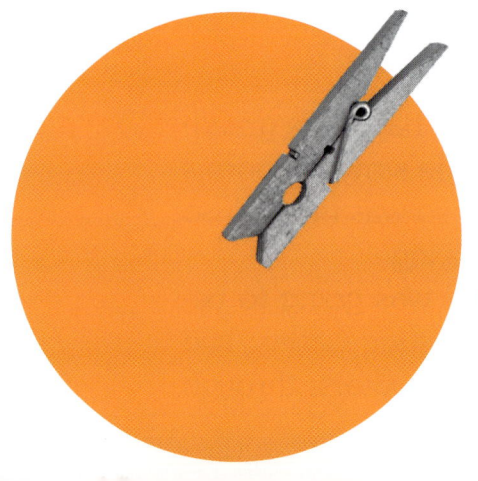

t h e n

Soft, fresh clothes, thanks to the natural outdoor breeze.

after that, on the one-year anniversary of their first date.

Then one night Casey came home and said, "Well, Mom and Dad, I've got good news and, uh, surprising news. Paula and I are definitely getting married. I've bought her ring, and we're engaged and everything. And, uh, the surprising news is that you're going be grandparents a whole lot sooner than we'd planned."

They had just found out that day that Paula was pregnant. As seems to happen with young couples these days, they were pregnant before they got married. We were very happy for them, and we said, "How do you and Paula feel about this?"

He said, "Oh, we're both really excited!"

Then we asked, "Well, how did this happen?"

He said, "Well, you know, the usual way."

"But was it intentional or . . . accidental?"

He said, "Well, we weren't using any kind of birth control. We decided we would just, you know, let God be in charge. We both wanted to be parents. We both wanted to have a baby."

That's how we found out. When they got married, Paula was about six months pregnant, and Donovan was born shortly thereafter. Casey and Paula were 24 and 26 at the time. Donovan is 3½ now.

I was there when Donovan was born. In fact, I was also the one who went shopping with Paula for a wedding gown and helped her pick out the veil. I got to be the mother of the bride, and then I got to be the grandmother of the newborn! My husband wasn't there, but I was, and my son was in the delivery room with his wife. They had an emergency C-section due to complications. Then Casey brought Donovan into the glassed-in room where they had the warmers. He showed him to me in the window, and I just cried my heart out. They were tears of happiness—I was so overwhelmed by looking at my son and my grandson and seeing this eternal progression.

You know, they say your children are your footsteps in the sands of eternity. Well, so are your grandchildren, and it was a very moving moment to see three generations of us looking at one another through this glass window. Casey laid the baby in the warmer and was putting the little booties on him, and he had all the earmarks immediately of being a wonderful father.

As I was watching the two of them through the window, I realized that becoming a grandparent just opens up a whole new door into your heart—you didn't even know it was there!—and all of a sudden this light comes flooding in and you realize there's a whole new type of love you've never experienced before.

You have love for your parents, and you have love for yourself as a child and for your siblings and then for your friends. You eventually have romantic love for a boyfriend, and then you have marital love for your spouse—every love is so different. Then you have the love for your own children, which you think will make your heart explode because it's so overwhelming and all consuming.

But then a grandchild comes along. I was so startled to experience this new kind of love. It's completely different from the love you feel for your children or your spouse or your parents. It's an entirely new realm of love, a new door opening into your heart. And it continues to be overwhelming, as you can tell.

My husband feels exactly the same way. We've talked about it often, about how it's stunning in its difference. It's very difficult to explain. It's a wonderful new world of emotion—the love that you have for this grandchild.

JEANNE C.
Los Vegas, Nevada

now

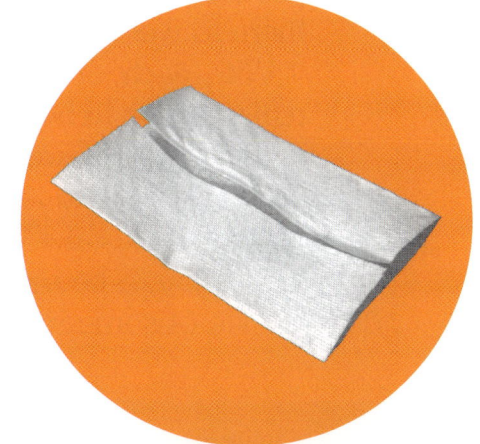

Industrially softened, artificially scented clothes, thanks to the miracle of dryer sheets.

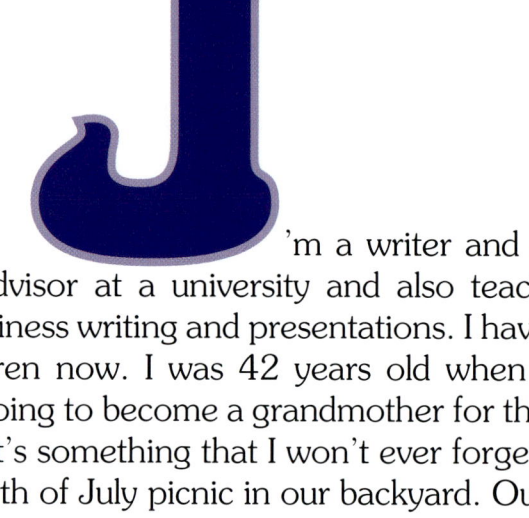

'm a writer and a presentation advisor at a university and also teach seminars in business writing and presentations. I have five grandchildren now. I was 42 years old when I learned I was going to become a grandmother for the first time, and it's something that I won't ever forget. It was at a Fourth of July picnic in our backyard. Our daughter and her husband had surprised us with a visit. They shared the news as we were sitting outside getting ready to enjoy a little July 4th celebration. The timing was fun, because my birthday is July 7. It was a dual celebration that year!

I was so excited about it—and more than just over-whelmed. I felt then, as I have with each grandchild since, that our family was handpicked by that child. I guess this idea or this image that I held of being picked by that child gave it a special feeling. I was there to welcome and await the arrival.

With each of my grandchildren, I've seen it as a real privilege to be a grandparent. I have two fabulous daughters who are proving to be fabulous mothers, but I always have felt that grandparenting is the icing on top of the cake, or the cherries on the sundae. It's such a joy to be a grandparent and to be involved in the life of someone who shares your DNA, who carries certain little elements of you around and who will be there when you might not be there any longer.

JANET C.
Princeton Junction, New Jersey

y first grandchild was born 12 years ago. My stepdaughter called and said, "I have some really wild news! I'm pregnant!" And I thought, "This is good. She sounds happy. She wants to be a mom." I felt like it was a real transition. She wasn't a girl anymore. Now she was a real woman. She was 24 at that time.

There was a bit of a transition for me too. It was new territory, and a new experience for me to think that there was a baby and I was not the mom but the grandmother. Even these days, when I go out with my grandchildren, everybody thinks I'm their mother—and I adore that, because it's like my stepchildren have done all the hard work but I get the credit! I'm very happy that I'm a young grandmother. I think that the kids like it, and there are fewer rules we have to observe because I'm physically able to do anything a parent would do.

MECHELE F.
New York, New York

n my work as a Reiki practitioner, I am in the alternative healing field and am also an aromatherapist and refloxologist.

My first grandchild was a grandson. When we learned that he was going to be born, there was that realization that you're no longer 30 years old, which may have been a fun, free-living time even though you had children. Now you realize that your children are having children, so it "cements" where you are in your life. Being 42 and finding out I was having a grandchild brought those mixed emotions, where you go from "Oh my goodness, I'm not that age any-more!" to "Oh, how fantastic! Now there's going to be someone to love beyond my children." I had lost my own parents at a relatively young age; I was 22. My dad was a private pilot, and he and my mother were both killed in his plane. I realized that my parents wouldn't be there to see their grandchild born, and I thought, "There's something else they're going to miss out on." But I was also really ecstatic. It's almost surreal the first time you find out that you're going to be a grandparent. I think it takes several months before it fully hits you. Then when you see your child is actually pregnant, you think, "Oh my gosh, this is actually real. There's a baby on the way!"

I used to live in Santa Barbara, California, and only

saw my grandchildren once a week or once a month. Being an independent contractor, I also worked on call for some of the high-end hotels in Santa Barbara. One of my biggest accounts closed down for a remodeling project. So, I decided to make a move to San Clemente to be close to my grandchildren. Now I'm only minutes from them, and I help my daughter out. I watch my grandkids all day Monday. I also used to come over on either Saturday night or Sunday night, so my daughter and son-in-law could have a night out, which I think is really important in a relationship when you have young children.

Now my younger daughter, my baby, is expecting a child; she's due in August. She lives in Santa Barbara County, and I'm reevaluating—again—where I am right now. Perhaps I'll go back to Ventura County to be close to my daughter and my newest grandchild, who's on the way. Being an independent contractor is really nice, because it gives me the ability to set my own hours and to be where I want, and need, to be.

HEIDI W.
San Clemente, California

 am first and foremost a real estate investor and a real estate investing trainer. I also own a direct mail company for helping businesses develop repeat and referral business through the use of direct mail. On occasion, I do event planning, and I've produced several major events in Las Vegas—a Shakespeare festival, and a jazz festival. Most importantly, I'm a full-time grandma, with nine grandkids all over the country. My husband and I try to stay in touch with them on a weekly basis. It takes up a lot of time, but it's time well spent and it's one of the most nourishing things in our life.

When I first learned that I was going to be a grandparent, it wasn't the storybook experience that we all probably hope to have. My daughter was an amazing student. She was an honor roll student, voted valedictorian. She was a cheerleader and was homecoming queen—and suddenly, at 16 years old she announced to me that she was madly in love, pregnant, and she was going to get married.

At first, all my hopes and dreams for her came crashing down and my heart broke. Then I realized that she has to walk her path the way she is creating it. She's an intelligent girl, and somehow we would make it through this. I didn't know at that time what decisions she would make. We had to sit down and have a long talk about what being a parent looks like and the fact that it's a lifelong commitment. I talked her through the alternatives and choices—abortion, adoption, all of them very painful to consider—and none of them really felt quite right because of the timing in her life. I knew that no matter what decision she made, it was going to be a very hard one. But ultimately she decided that she was going to marry this young man and that she was going to have this baby, and so I settled in with her choice.

Then we decided that we were going to move forward and celebrate this baby and be happy about this experience. I don't know that I really understood at that point what it was going to be like to be a grandparent. I was more focused on how to help my daughter and how to be a support to her through the huge decision she was making. It wasn't until Tesha was born that I could really experience it.

I was in the radio business at that time, and Tesha was born on St. Patrick's Day. We did live promotions at different places around the city. I happened to be at a huge Irish bar, as a promotion for our radio station, when I got the call that my daughter had gone into labor. I was so excited to get to the hospital, and a whole bunch of my friends came with me.

We got there just after the baby was born—it happened very quickly—and I remember seeing Tesha as they rolled her into the nursery. I got to look through the glass and see her for the first time. She had the most beautiful, wide-open eyes. I'd never seen a newborn so alert and so intent on studying her surroundings. The minute I looked into her eyes, I knew that we were going to have a unique and very special relationship; it was a very powerful moment for me. I am at a loss for words to describe it. It was a moment when you realize that part of you is now moving forward and creating new people, new generations, new families—it's a very, very powerful experience to see your first grandchild for the first time.

SUZAN H.
Las Vegas, Nevada

J'm a real estate executive with a major firm in Chicago. Now I live part of the year in Tucson, which is a wonderful escape from the Chicago winters I've known all my life.

When I think about being a grandparent, I always remember the relationship I had with my grandmother and the big role she played in my life. Her role actually got bigger as she got older—and she lived to be 103! She was a graduate of the University of Chicago, she'd seen Easy Rider in her 80s, and she was reading Kurt Vonnegut books when she was in her 90s. She was very open-minded, and she always wanted to discuss things with my sister and me.

For whatever reason, my parents were not as involved with my two daughters—their grandchildren—as my grandmother had been with me, or as I want to be with my grandchildren. The way our family has

then

Blue Plate Special:
nutritious, lots of flavor.

developed is fairly unusual, I think. My older daughter had some serious health problems between the ages of six and twelve. She had a form of colitis that required more than a dozen major operations. Treating her illness dominated the life of our family for five or six years, and even afterward she had to be watched very carefully. Obviously it was very difficult for her, and it also was difficult for her younger sister—there were times when she started to feel pretty lost.

Now both my daughters are married. My younger daughter has just made me a new grandfather, and the older one is going to do the same very soon. This is happening in different ways, however. My younger daughter gave birth to a baby girl, and my older daughter and her husband are going to be adopting a baby girl from China. As things worked out, one baby was born just as my older daughter and her husband are getting ready to depart for China to get their baby girl. We're getting two grandchildren—at the same time!—by very different routes.

There are a lot of new feelings at a time like this. When you see a baby just born, you definitely feel older for a while. But that's not an entirely unpleasant feeling. It's kind of nice to see your children in the role of parent that you occupied for so long. You can say, "Now it's your turn!" Of course, it isn't only their turn, and my wife and I are looking forward to being very close to the new members of our family. We just want to emphasize the fun a little more and the responsibility a little less.

We believe it was probably the effects of my older daughter's surgeries that prevented her from becoming pregnant. Obviously, everyone has been disappointed for her, and there were times during her younger sister's pregnancy that she felt really low.

The health problems she had for so many years were very difficult, and she's still feeling the effects. Having said that, it's also hugely exciting to be adopting from China, and it's a real innovation for our family. For many generations we have married within the same geographical and ethnic categories. Our gene pool is really going to change now! And it's great to know that my older daughter, who went through so much herself, will be able to help a little girl—who was put out on the street in China—to have a better life. We've seen enough pain and unhappiness in children. We're all ready to move things in the opposite direction.

MURRAY W.
Chicago, Illinois

have two grandchildren—Ben, who is almost two now, and Samantha, who is now nine weeks old. Our daughter and son-in-law surprised us. We were having a family gathering of some sort, and my son-in-law and I were talking about gardening. He said, "Well, we're going to have something in bloom in the early summer." I was wondering, "I wonder what he means? What kind of plant could he be talking about?" And then Barbara, my wife, started screaming, "Oh my God! Oh my God!" She immediately understood what was going on—and at that point we all went absolutely nuts.

When you first hear something like that, you just think, "Wow, this is what life is all about." You don't worry about anything. You just think that this is the payoff for having children and for having a great family. And it hasn't really changed since then, except it's just gotten better and better. In fact, I have to be careful, because I don't want people to think I'm just a blathering idiot when I start talking about my grandchildren. So maybe it's best that I only communicate with other grandparents, because they understand instantly what I'm talking about!

LARRY K.
New York, New York

now

Complete meal bar:
nutritious, no flavor.

ight now I don't feel any older than I ever have. I feel just the same as always, or maybe even better. I don't think people look at me any differently either. Occasionally, though, my husband mentions that two of his grandkids are almost grown up—and then I see people starting to "do the math": "Well, if they're this age, then she must be that age…" I love those kids, they're beautiful inside and out, but I wish grandchildren didn't turn into calculators for estimating people's age!

The truth is I've never really felt comfortable with the word "grandmother." It makes me think of my own grandmother, who couldn't see very well and who had a stooped over walk. That's not how I am at all, so when my daughter Ginger had her first child I suggested that Ray ought to call me something different. When Ray was old enough to start talking, Ginger decided on Grammy as a name for me—which I thought was fine, but Ray refused to say it. Somehow he came up with Monnie. That was great, and now all seven of my grandchildren call me Monnie. I really love it, because it's a name that's only for me.

That wasn't the only time that something remarkable happened concerning names. When my son Scott and his wife were going to have their first child, we all started thinking about what the name should be. There were a lot of suggestions, but we weren't really able to come up with a name that everyone liked. Finally Scott said, "Well, this is our child and we're going to pick the name." He was right of course, and I completely accepted it. But then they went away on vacation, and I had an amazing dream. I dreamed that my new granddaughter appeared to me and I asked her name. She said, "My name is Brittany." When I woke up I told Rick that I had dreamed the perfect name. He liked it too, but we knew that we had agreed to go with the name that they would pick. When Scott and his wife came back from their vacation, they said, "Well, we've picked a name." Rick and I were ready for anything, but then they said, "We're going to name her Britney!" We couldn't believe it, because this was long before Brittany was a popular name.

SONJA P.
Oceanside, California

What do these names have in common?

Alex Ali Andy Angel Ashton Avery
Bailey Bobby Blair Brook Cameron Casey
Charlie Chris Dale Drew Gale Jamie Jerry
Jessie Jody Joey Jordan Justice Kris
Lindsey Logan Lonnie Madison Markie Max
Morgan Nick Pat Phoenix Riley Ryan Sam
Sandy Skyler Taylor Tony Tracy Tyler

Find the answer in the back of this book...and go to
www.grandparentsrock.com for more quizzes, trivia and other fun stuff!

What have your grandchildren brought into your life and the life of your family?

With all the oddities and wonderment, these new arrivals invariably bring excitement, love, newness—and, above all, change—at a time when things might have been becoming just a bit too settled. Many new grandparents are shaken by this, a few may be rattled for a moment, and some just roll on through. In fact, at various times you may experience all three of these feelings. But you'll have time to reflect on all this later. Right now, get out in that kitchen and rattle those pots and pans!

GRANDPARENT GUIDELINES

* As you get older, be aware of what happens if you just keep living as you always have. To the world, it will look like you're slowing down. Being a grandparent is a great way to take your life up a notch, so make the most of it!

* Remember that judging our parents (or our children) doesn't solve anything. Take responsibility! Life has funny ways of teaching us lessons we need to learn

* Accept change with humor, and embrace change with love

NOTES

36

Grandparents ROCK

45 RPM

girls just want to have fun

To one who doesn't hear the music,
the dancers always look crazy.

Sufi proverb

CHAPTER 2

girls just want to have fun

38

This chapter is all about discovering endless ways to have fun with our grandkids. After all, girls do want to have fun—and so do boys! Having raised two daughters, I know about playing with Barbie's, dress up and make-believe. But finding ways to have fun with grandson Dylan has been a completely new experience. Army men and Pokemon card games were as foreign to me as running a marathon.

I'm sure Cindy Lauper never imagined her hit song from the '80s would be featured in a book for grandparents. But things do change; and as you get older, becoming a grandparent is definitely a change for the better. The trick is learning to make the most of it.

One afternoon Dylan and I went to Soup Plantation for an early dinner. He was having his usual chicken noodle soup, Jell-O and slice of pizza, while I enjoyed a volcano-sized plate of salad. I've never been able to go through their buffet line and come out with a reasonable amount of salad on my plate. It always ends up piled too high, looking as though it could feed two people.

While Dylan ate his fifth serving of Jell-O, I checked out the contents of his ever-present toy bag. He had about a hundred little green plastic army figures, some Transformer characters of the super hero type, a few little bouncy balls and parts of God knows what else. I pulled out a few of the green Army guys and began placing them in formation about the table. Little by little, I saw the beginnings of a battle scene. Soon we had army guys positioned on top of napkin holders and soup bowls. Shredded carrots from my salad became beachfront sand, and broccoli turned into bushes. We had such a colorful display that a small crowd formed around our table. Sounds really silly, doesn't it? Well, so what! You're a grandparent. This part of your life is made for being outrageous.

For me, another fun-food-escape trip was McDonald's, which always provided more than a meal. Children love the food, and now, with their selection of salads and some other healthy choices, the rest of us can eat there too. When Dylan was a toddler, taking him to McDonald's for a plain hamburger and French fries always provided 30 minutes of solo active playtime in the fully contained playground. I would sit and watch with the joyful realization that his naptime would be guaranteed. His naps were a necessity for me; my work as a consultant required a couple of uninterrupted hours of either talking on the telephone or researching on the Web. Consider a trip to McDonald's with your grandkids: It's great fun and affordably feeds both of you in an environment kids love—and it wears them out!

On the days when you're feeling more energetic, swimming, going to the beach or building indoor forts will help you build a memorable relationship with your grandkids. On my Web site www.grandparentsrock.com, you'll find pictures and downloadable instructions for some spectacular tents Dylan and I created. I hope you'll go there and feel inspired.

Spending time, playing and talking with Dylan brings me more joy than I ever imagined possible, along with the freedom to love completely. Of course, there was great love raising my two daughters and there was some fun, but mostly there was the responsibility of raising future good citizens. This required discipline and disciplining. I'm proud to say my girls did well in school, both achieving bachelor of science and master's degrees. As a grandparent, I now have the freedom and privilege to love completely. Being with my grandchild reminds me of the often-quoted sentiment "If I'd known grandkids would be such fun, I would have had them first."

y wife and I have five grandchildren, from the ages of five to 14. We also have two little "adopted" grandchildren, Shivani and Khushani, whose family is from India. We play the role of grandparent for them, which is really a lot of fun.

Once, we were with Shivani in the car when she was about two years old, and we were all just talking silly. For some reason the word picnic came up, and she wanted to know what it meant. So we explained that it's a kind of party, and you eat outside. So she asked, "Well, what do you eat?" We told her that you eat all kinds of stuff, like candy and sandwiches, and even lizards and snakes!

From that moment on, she couldn't get the idea of a picnic out of her mind. Every time she saw us and every time we talked on the phone, she would say, "When are we going on a picnic? When are we going on a picnic?" So we finally packed up some stuff and went down on the grass and had one. I don't know if it was as exciting as she thought it would be, but at least we finally did it!

RICK M.
Oceanside, California

onovan loves music, and I like to think it goes back to when he was a newborn and I did a lot of babysitting. Whenever I had Donovan, I would put on Sergeant Pepper's Lonely Hearts Club Band or the Bee Gees and I would dance him to sleep. In my work with children's multimedia projects I write a lot of original music, so Donovan and I like to make up silly songs together, with a lot of rhyme. The basic building blocks of childhood literacy are rhyme, rhythm and repetition. So from the time he was a newborn, I would sing songs to him, make up silly poems for him and do everything in rhyme and rhythm. Donovan picked it up too as soon as he started talking. One of his favorite books is Fox in Socks. It's a Dr. Seuss book, and it's full of alliteration and silly rhyme.

We play rhyming games in the car, making rhymes out of nothing. You know, a poodle eating noodles in a puddle in a muddle, which is part of Fox in Socks. We also do a lot of reading and on-the-floor play, whether it's Lego's or drawing or crayons or Etch-a-Sketch. So Donovan gets a lot of verbal stimulation, a lot of artistic stimulation—drawing and crayons and paper—and tons of music.

JEANNE C.
Las Vegas, Nevada

ome of my earliest memories of Dylan start at my beach cottage when he was a toddler. I loved (and still do) to play with him on the sand, build sand castles, dig for crabs, swim in the tide and wave at big boats as they were sailing or motoring from Newport Harbor just moments before entering the ocean waters. One of my favorite pictures is of Dylan at 20 months walking across the sand toward the water in his diapered swim trunks and with his bucket. We still love to go to the beach and dig holes, build sand castles and swim in the ocean together.

PAT B.
Newport Beach, California

ith my grandson, who's almost two, we really like to play hoops. As a former high school basketball player, I'm really delighted. We have a basket set up at his height in his parents' living room, and we have a variety of balls that he likes to use, usually two at a time. He has all sorts of shots he likes to try: banking the ball off the backboard and also dunking it. That's been a lot of fun for both of us.

Of course, I also love to read to him. His parents have done a great job of teaching him the alphabet and getting him interested in books. It's fun to watch day by day as he's able to grasp more and more information. For me, that's without a doubt one of the most exciting things I get to see taking place. I think

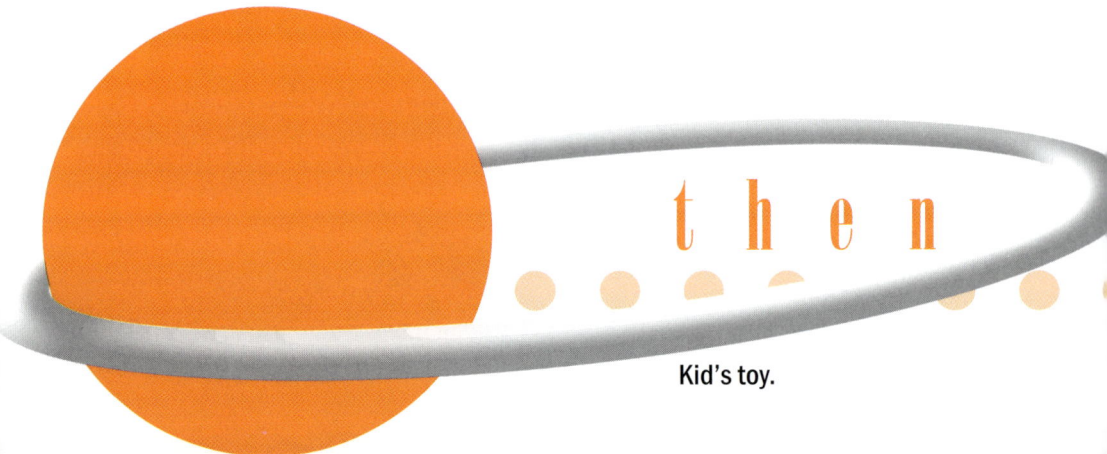

t h e n

Kid's toy.

Ben is moving very quickly in his learning, and the basketball games are a great way of helping him to enjoy physical activity too.

LARRY K.
New York, New York

t's way more fun to have the grandchildren visiting without the parents. They just act differently when their parents are away. I act differently too, because I can stop worrying that I'm going to do something the parents don't like.

An interesting aspect of being a grandparent for the first time is learning the pecking order, so to speak. You've raised your kids, and you have certain ways that you talked with them or disciplined them—but now they are the parents and not just the kids anymore. There's also your son-in-law or your daughter-in-law, who may not want you to be parenting their kids. So you learn really quickly to shut your mouth; your wisdom isn't always welcomed.

With my grandkids, I get down on the floor and I crawl around with them and we play make-believe. We pretend there are lions and tigers, and I growl with them, just to let them know it's okay to have that kind of imagination. We also enjoy being outside. I love to garden, so they garden right along with me. We plant flowers and pick weeds, and I teach them about nature, about butterflies and hummingbirds and being able to experience it. I think parents often get too busy and don't have time for things like that. I think that's a fun role to have as grandparents to just get down to the very basic things.

ḤEIDI W.
San Clemente, California

y   oldest grandson, Brennan, is a wonderful hockey player. We are a "stick-and-ball" family, and hockey is a big sport with us. I have played a lot of hockey with Brennan. He used to conduct little hockey clinics for Grammy and teach me all the specific moves. Once he said to me, "Not every grandmother plays hockey with her grandson!" Certainly he was much better than I was, but I was at least a willing student in his hockey clinic from a very early time. I've played lots of outdoor activities with all my grandchildren—whatever the child is interested in doing. The almost-three-year-old just loves to be on playgrounds, and he has a keen imagination. When you're reading a book, he likes to pretend that he's in the book doing whatever is happening in the book, so we sort of jump in together and become whatever is going on in that story.

Grandchildren like to teach us, and they take pride in doing that. I think they just love the fact that the grandparent is a willing recipient. We have taken our grandson on intergenerational Elderhostel trips. We were talking to some of the grandparents, and one of them said, "Do you think this would be the same extraordinary experience if the parents were along?" We all immediately said no, because anytime that just grandparents and grandchildren hang out, it's completely different. The children have wonderful parents, but it's the grandparents who have all the "no agenda" time. As grandparents, we don't have to be responsible for their overall upbringing. Yet I think we also have a great influence on how they do turn out.

JANET C.
Princeton Junction, New Jersey

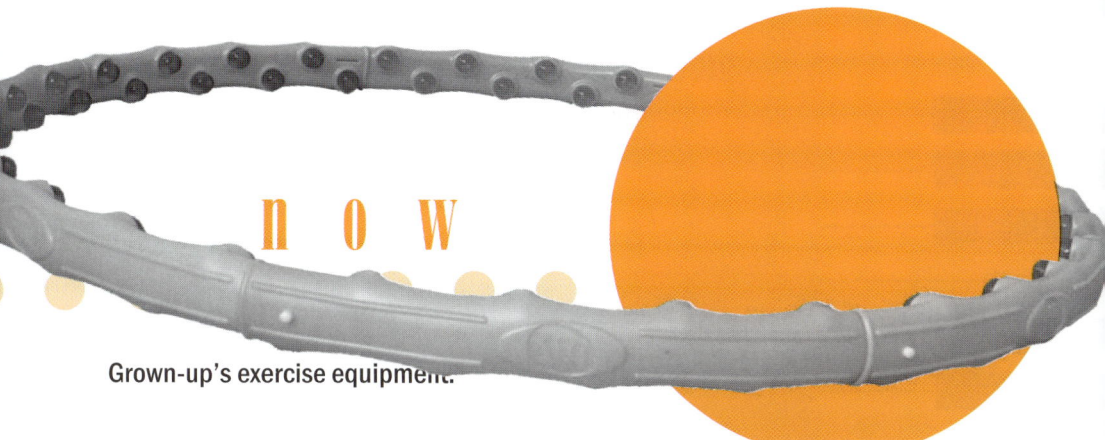

N O W

Grown-up's exercise equipment.

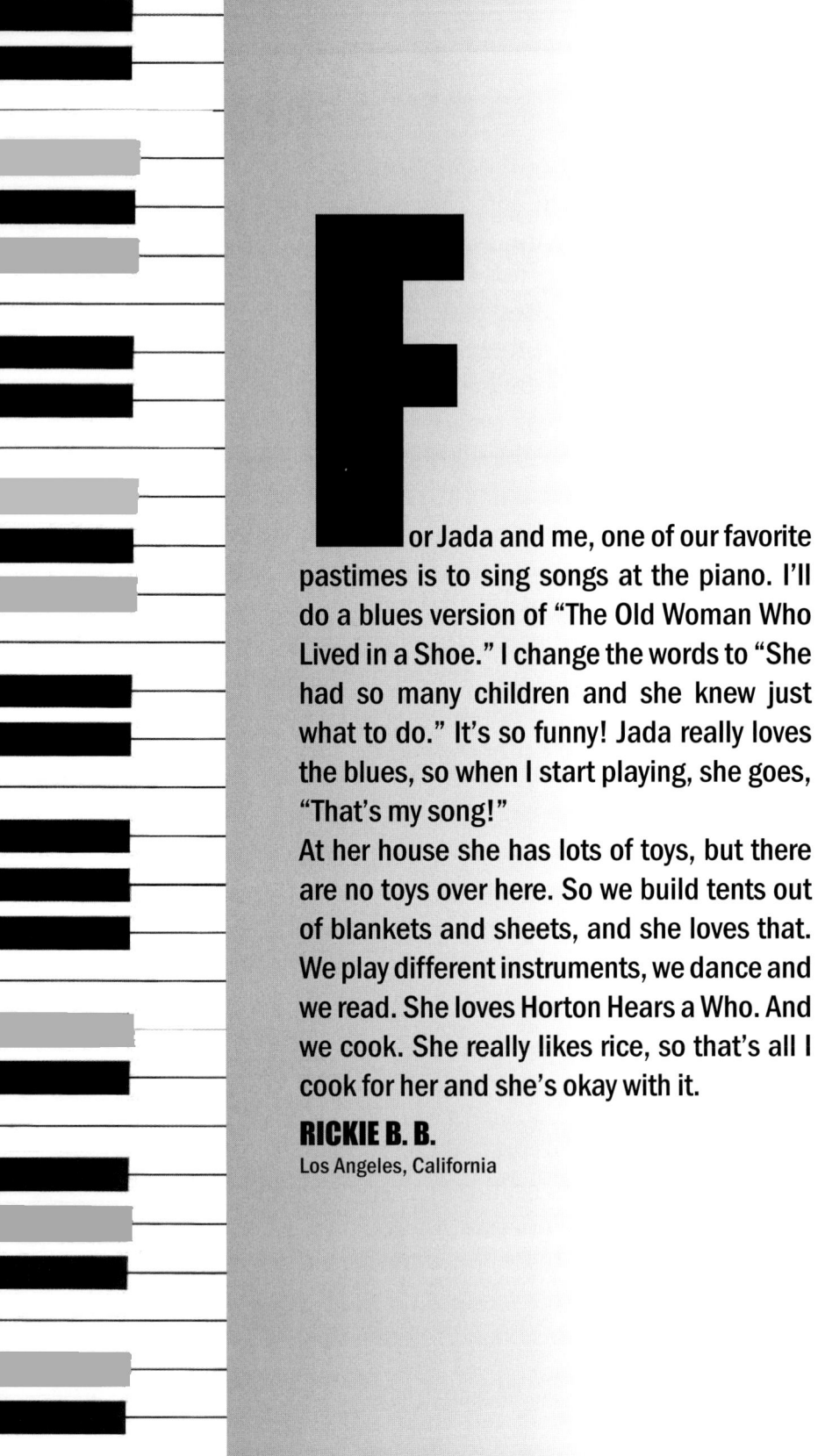

For Jada and me, one of our favorite pastimes is to sing songs at the piano. I'll do a blues version of "The Old Woman Who Lived in a Shoe." I change the words to "She had so many children and she knew just what to do." It's so funny! Jada really loves the blues, so when I start playing, she goes, "That's my song!"

At her house she has lots of toys, but there are no toys over here. So we build tents out of blankets and sheets, and she loves that. We play different instruments, we dance and we read. She loves Horton Hears a Who. And we cook. She really likes rice, so that's all I cook for her and she's okay with it.

RICKIE B. B.
Los Angeles, California

We are a very creative, fun, active family; and when the grandkids visit, we do all kinds of things. One of the activities they really like to do with me is paint birdhouses. I buy unpainted, unfinished birdhouses at Michael's, and I always have them here for whenever the kids come over. And usually one of the first questions they ask when they walk in the door is "Can we paint birdhouses?"

In our last home, we had a room that was specifically the grandchildren's room, and on the walls we had put up white picket fences. We had painted the walls a light blue like the sky, with clouds painted on them. Every time the kids made birdhouses, we would attach them to the picket fence. They loved that room. It was their room, and it had their signature all over it. That was great fun. Also, I'm a potter. The grandkids love to come over and learn how to build clay pots on the wheel. Then, by their next visit, I've fired their projects so they're ready to paint.

What else do we do? We really love to pretend. One night when I had all the grandkids over, we put up tents in the backyard. We called them teepees, not tents—and we entered into a pretend world. For the whole night, we pretended we were Native Americans. We were a tribe of people going fishing in the big cement pond, the "g r e a t lake." I brought brooms and hung strings off the ends, and we pre-tended there was a hook on the end of each string. Then we'd fish our dinner out of the lake. I had bought fish earlier in the day, and so we cooked it over the fire, telling stories about our adventures that day. It was so amazing to hear these children go into such a creative world and truly comprehend what it would be like to live in a primi-tive environment. I was delighted in the way they de-scribed their days: hunting, seeing elk on the horizon, grinding up the corn for the meal. They told me these really remarkable stories of things that had happened to them all day that were, of course, all make-believe. That was a night that I don't think any of us will forget, a very power-ful, creative experience that we had together.

We also go "quadding" quite a bit. A quad is a four-wheeled all-terrain vehicle. Living out in the rural area outside Las Vegas, we can go out on the quads, around the wall of the house, and we're literally off in the desert exploring for treasures.

One of the things that I've been doing for years is collecting heart-shaped rocks, so the grandkids are always scouring the desert looking for rocks that are shaped like hearts. If they're big, we bring them back and put them in the garden. If they're small, we put them in what I call the Zen box, which is a big wooden box full of sand, with a light in it, displayed in my living room. It's amazing to watch the kids when they visit because they know the rule: Only one person at a time can sit at the Zen box. That's their quiet time to create and draw pictures in the sand. And it's the one time that I don't see the kids bickering over whose turn it is. They just seem to have this sense and know that when one of them is sitting at the Zen box, the others need to stay away. It's that child's turn to be at the Zen box; and when they're done, they'll get their turn.

When my grandkids were really young, of course, they would just want to go over and make a big mess in the Zen box. They would start digging through the sand and throw things everywhere. So I had to sit each one of them down and explain to them that this was their time to be quiet and to draw or express in the sand what was in their heart: a quiet time for their heart to "talk" to the earth. I had to sit with them one by one and teach them how to experience the feeling of working with a Zen box; it didn't take them long to get it. You can see when they have the "Aha!" because they become very quiet. They just start moving things around in the box and drawing. They become very, very quiet. That's when you know to gently tiptoe away and leave them in their experience.

I've always been a bit of a thrill seeker, so one of the things that I taught my granddaughter to do early on was to climb trees. One day her mom arrived while the two of us were sitting all the way up in this big tree in my front yard. We were having a great time telling stories. It turned out not to be such a wonderful moment, though. My daughter was very upset with me for teaching Tesha to climb this tree; but I couldn't help remembering what an absolutely fun experience it was for me when I was a child to crawl up into trees. It's almost like you're hiding, but you're not. You're so high up, you can see the world; and it's a really interesting vantage point for a child. I really had enjoyed teaching my granddaughter that experience. But I quickly learned it wasn't what my daughter wanted me to be doing. I trust her decision and understand it, so I had to start figuring out how to be a fun grandmother while still staying within the parameters that my daughter wished for her daughter.

Another time, I bought my granddaughter a wagon for her birthday. It was already assembled, and I couldn't figure out how to wrap it. So I went to the store and bought about 10 or 15 giant-sized bags of M&M'S, filled the whole wagon with them and put a big bow on the handle. It was very colorful and festive and celebratory. Well, that didn't go over well with my daughter either, because the first thing she thought was "Oh my gosh, all this sugar, all this chocolate." Oops! I had to convince her that she could bag up all the M&M'S, because they keep forever, and that she could dole them out as she wished. She could look at it as she's got ten years' worth of Easter basket candy. But really this time, I didn't care. It was just a method for me to make the wagon a big surprise. That was how I started learning to navigate the waters with my daughter in terms of what was okay and wasn't okay for me to do with my grandchildren.

SUZAN H.
Las Vegas, Nevada

 think life happens in stages. You're a child, you're an adult; there's the crawling stage, there's the walking stage. And the same thing happens when you're with your grandchildren. Right now, we are at the cooking stage, which is from five to 11 years old. They look forward to coming to Gaga's, and we really cook. We're not just baking cookies. We are making pancakes, flipping them over on the griddle, we're cracking our eggs into the little rings. My 13-year-old came over Friday. His sister and I had purchased three ripe avocados, and we made guacamole. We tore some tortillas to make chips and quick-fried them in a little bit of oil. There was enough so that everyone had a full cup of guacamole made with cut-up onion and tomatoes, some cilantro, some lemon juice, salt and pepper. We've also done the finger painting thing, which is great. If you use a floor tile for your base for the kids to paint, then if you like it, you can keep it; if you don't, you can just wash it off. White is best, a white ceramic tile.

SYDNEY B.
Tulsa, Oklahoma

NOTES

54

y two oldest grandchildren love to build and assemble things. Their favorite color is orange because that's the Home Depot color. To them, a vacation is going to Home Depot and being able to walk around and see all the cool tools. I've made a special place where I have a house that's constructed out of foam rubber. It's big, and you can assemble it in different ways. We like to see how we can put it together; once it's together, then they love to destroy it. They think that's great!

LEE B.
Salt Lake City, Uah

56

y favorite time with my grandchildren is when we have our "pretend birthdays." Two years ago I sent cards to my grandchildren that included coupons for a pretend birthday. Using this coupon, they could decide when their pretend birthday would be, what they wanted to do and how old they were going to be. Of course, it wasn't surprising that they both wanted their pretend birthday to be as soon as possible, so we booked Bryden's pretend birthday for Friday and Teanna's for Saturday!

Bryden, who was nine at the time, decided he wanted to be 15 for his pretend birthday and asked if he could bring a "girlfriend." His wish was to go to a restaurant and order a steak—something he'd never done before—and then go to Rucker's, a gaming ar-

then

Metal skate, metal wheels, and a metal key to wear as a medallion around your neck.

cade. As an added surprise, I secretly hired a limousine to pick up Bryden and his friend, chauffeur them through the park and drop them off at the restaurant. They were both absolutely beaming when the limo pulled up at the restaurant.

I arrived at the restaurant before them, dropped off candles for the cake and let the owner know that it was a "pretend birthday." Halfway through Bryden's steak, the owner came by the table, introduced himself, shook Bryden's hand and wished him a happy "15th" birthday. The owner then agreed to pose for pictures with the kids. Following dinner and cake, we topped off the night playing games and winning tokens at Rucker's.

Teanna was five at the time and chose to be 10 for her pretend birthday. Her wish was to go to Boston Pizza for "Bugs and Cheese," then visit the toy store and end the celebration at Rucker's.

We had such a great time that a few days later, Teanna called and said, "Grandma, I think we should have another pretend birthday." I told her I agreed and that I wanted a pretend birthday, too. She thought that was a good idea until I told her I wanted to be five, her current age. She tried to convince me that I should be "27, like my mom," or alternatively "17, like Jennifer, my babysitter." I couldn't get her to agree to let me be five.

A few weeks later I was turning 50, and my family

fulfilled my "pretend birthday" wish by turning the numbers in my age around and giving me a fifth birthday! The string of balloons across my sister's backyard all announced my "new" age! A Barbie doll cake was in the center of the table—with hidden treasures of money and toys baked inside! And as I opened my presents, which included bubbles, sidewalk chalk, a Barbie doll and a beautiful china tea set, Teanna leaned over to me and exclaimed, "Oh, Grandma, you're so lucky!"

Needless to say, pretend birthdays have become part of our tradition, and it's always a delight to discover what age the grandkids want to be and to see what that age represents to them.

Another ritual we have is adopting a family in need at Christmas time. My grandkids do all the shopping for the gifts and groceries, pick out the Christmas wrap, wrap all the presents and make homemade Christmas cards; and then we all go and deliver the package to the family. Throughout the entire process, it provides wonderful opportunities to talk about how we're all connected on this planet and need to take care of each other. It's amazing to hear from my grandkids the lessons they have learned from this: how important it is for us all to help each other, everyone should be happy at Christmas, not everyone has a mom and a dad, and how good it feels to give

to others. Invariably, when we deliver the baskets of food and gifts, we are all beaming with smiles as much as the family we are helping. **RHONDA B**.
Qu'Appelle, SK, Canada

The twins love to play with balls. We're always tossing balls, and recently they learned to kick them really well. They have a little pit with balls in it, and they love to play in there. I love to play with them there too, because they get so excited and it's so much fun. And also, ever since

N O W

Carbon fiber boot, polyeurethane wheels, shock absorbers, velcro straps, nylon brakes, and LED safety lights.

they were babies they've loved the peek-a-boo game. Even now that they're older, I'll hide around the corner and peek out, and they just crack up laughing. Little Tommy is four now and loves to go to the park; that's a big treat. Also, he loves to play with chalk. I've bought chalk in all different colors for him to use when he visits. We have a huge driveway, and by the time he leaves, it is just covered with chalk drawings. We've done flowers, balloons, butterflies and happy faces. Even the simplest things, and the least expensive, can be so much fun.

JANE M.
Azusa, California

very time I went over to see my grandkids, I'd pack a bag for each of them. And boy, they eyed that bag when they realized that every time Nonie comes over, there's something in that bag. One time my daughter said to Matthew, "You have to at least say hi to Nonie before you ask what's in the bag." This has kind of turned into our joke.

When Matt was a little baby, for some reason we called him Mattie Bear. Of course, that's gone away—but I still call him Bear. I always sang a song to him,

"You Are My Sunshine." He knows it word for word; and when we're together, he'll say, "Nonie, let's sing our song." And Rachel has it memorized now too. I call Rachel my little princess. Just today I bought her a couple of great little sweat suits and nightshirts with princesses all over the place. And now she's just like Matt, saying, "Nonie, Nonie, do you have my present?"

We do play a lot of games together. I just bought them checkers, Chinese checkers, and Tiddlywinks, of all things. I couldn't believe I found a Tiddlywinks game! We play all these kinds of games, and we also paint.

I'm also an elephant freak. I have collected elephants for 30 years. I even have a painted canvas done by an elephant painting with his trunk. My grandson always says to me, "Nonie, you promise that's mine when you die, isn't it?" I tell him, "Yes, that's yours." We go to the Oakland Zoo all the time. That's the one thing we do every time I visit them, because of the elephants. When they go shopping for my birthday, it's anything with elephants. The kids just can't look at one without saying, "Nonie would be so happy!" And get this: We've even ridden real elephants!

RAJNE T.
Fullerton, California

hen you're a parent and a grandparent too, there are several different roles you play, especially if you're still working, as I am. Depending on who you are at heart, some of those roles feel more authentic to you than others. For some reason I have an ability to totally regress with little kids when I play with them. I'm not bragging about it, but it's just something I've always been able to do and I've always felt at home with. Not only can I get down to their level, I can actually get below their level—so that they're laughing at me at the same time as they're laughing with me. I don't think of myself as an especially gifted person, but I'm really grateful for this knack because I've had a lot of fun with it.

If being silly with kids in that way doesn't come naturally to you, you're probably better off not trying it—not because it makes the kids uncomfortable, but mostly because you won't feel comfortable yourself. It certainly doesn't mean you can't have a lot of fun with your grandchildren. For instance, I always admired Mr. Rogers—the way kids responded to his TV show was really amazing. But Mr. Rogers never acted silly. He never tried to regress to their level. He didn't really talk to kids like they were adults, but it wasn't the way most people talk to kids either. It was just who he really was, and that's why it was so effective. That's why it was great.

When my daughters were little, I would get down on the floor and pretend I was a seal, and I'll probably do it also with my grandchildren in a year or so. I just have to be careful about my back!

MURRAY W.
Chicago, Illinois

 have such warm memories of my grandparents, and that's what I'm hoping to establish with my grandchildren. I realize now that my grandmother had the patience of a saint. She played store with me so many times, where you take things out of the cupboard and you put them on a table. Then the child buys things from the store, or sometimes the child is the storekeeper. We did this time and time again. It seems like for every grandchild this is a favorite game up until they are four or five, and then it sort of fades. Another game we play is "mystery tour." We don't tell them where we're taking them, and on the way we give them little hints. It's also a way of giving them some local history. Here in New York I like to take them on the subway. Children today don't really ride the subway much, but I love the subway. It's so noisy, and it's fast and really fun; so I'll take my grandchildren on the subway on the way to lunch or on the way to the park.

MECHELE F.
New York, New York

Got grandkids? Have fun!

This chapter has brought to life some totally groovy ideas for playing with your grandchildren: chalk on the sidewalk, building tents and forts, creating a rock collection and shooting hoops, to mention a few. Which was your favorite? With the 12-year span of my grandchildren's ages, I know I'll be referring to this chapter often as baby Skye becomes a toddler and just wants to have fun!

GRANDPARENT GUIDELINES

* Be a student of the child, and play within the child's agenda

* If your play activities get your grandchildren really riled up, calm them yourself and don't leave it to the parents to bring them back down

* When in doubt, play hide-and-seek!

* Please visit www.grandparentsrock.com and submit your own fun ideas, especially photos of your homemade tents and forts!

NOTES

Grandparents *ROCK*

45
R

EASIER SAID THAN DONE

Kindness is more important than wisdom,

and the recognition of this

is the beginning of wisdom.

Theodore Isaac Rubin

CHAPTER 3

EASIER SAID THAN DONE

68

It's a small world—except when our grandchildren live hundreds of miles away, as many do today. With such distances separating families, bonding with our grandchildren may be easier said than done. This is a relatively recent development. Until the 1950s, most extended American families lived together, not necessarily in the same house but at least in the same neighborhood or city. People stayed put. They identified with where they came from. For parents and grandparents—as well as children and grandchildren—this provided some huge benefits. Plenty of relatives were on hand to play all the different roles that family life demands. If somebody needed a break, there was somebody else ready to take over. If two people had an argument with someone, a third person could provide advice and counsel. One definition of grandparent was "always available babysitter."

Obviously, much has changed, and it hasn't necessarily made things easier. The proximity to our extended families that we might once have taken for granted has become the exception rather than the rule. Even so, there is a potential upside to this demographic shift. Today, a visit with grandparents can be a really special occasion—a chance for grandchildren to learn about family history, to develop real closeness with someone besides mom and dad, and to hear stories about what life was like when dinosaurs (like Elvis!) roamed the earth. All over the country, rock 'n' roll grandparents are dealing creatively with the geographical separations that have become commonplace. It may be easier said than done, but we can do it too!

My grandchildren live in Arizona. I'm in California, so I'm only an hour's flight away. But it's still different from being "on site" all the time, as my grandmother was for me. The key, I think, is to maintain closeness using all the amazing tools that are now available—especially email, instant messaging, sharing digital photographs, and, for the technologically inclined, even the use of webcams. But in the midst of all this, let's not forget the tremendous thrill kids feel when they get a letter or greeting card in the mail addressed just to them. When we create a mix of both cutting-edge and "old-fashioned" ways of staying in touch, we magnify the excitement of our in-person visits when they do take place.

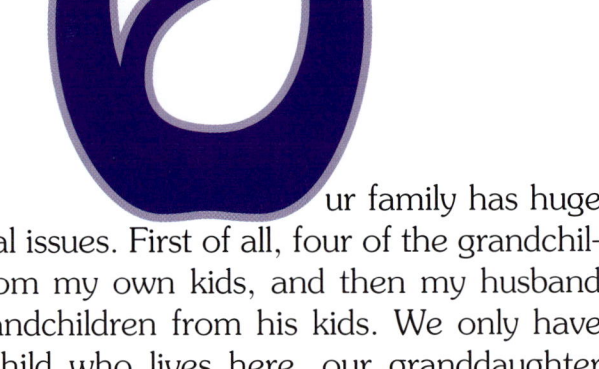ur family has huge geographical issues. First of all, four of the grandchildren are from my own kids, and then my husband has five grandchildren from his kids. We only have one grandchild who lives here, our granddaughter Katie. The rest live everywhere from Puerto Rico to New York to Texas to Arizona.

The holidays are the most difficult time, because most of our children are working, trying to build their careers, and they don't have surplus time or money to go on vacation. So, who do we spend the holidays with? Over the last couple of years, we have started planning our vacations to coincide with the holidays and we just invite everybody to come along. This has been a big transition for us, because both my husband and I are used to traditional holiday celebrations, but on the whole it's been really positive.

Last year for Thanksgiving we went to Hawaii. Several of our children came along and brought their kids, and we had a most amazing Thanksgiving. We actually went swimming with the dolphins on Thanksgiving Day, and that was great fun. Then, we planned Christmas in New York City, and again, some of the family joined us. We went to see the windows and the lights on Fifth Avenue, and we skated in Central Park and had a really great time.

But we still haven't arrived at a perfect solution. If we are with my kids, then his kids feel hurt. If we see his kids, then my kids feel hurt. We can't seem to get them to realize that we can't be everywhere at once. During the course of the year, we try to see everybody at least once and spend time specifically with our grandchildren. Meanwhile, we call them every week or send cards or letters or little gifts. We're constantly reaching out to each one of them.

SUZAN H.
Las Vegas, Nevada

hen Dylan was 10 years old, he and I went on our first trip together. I took him to Orlando to see Disney World and to visit my dad—his great-grandfather—and Betty Lou, my dad's wife. We managed to get our own row on a Southwestern Airlines flight, and played and read our way across the country on that very long trip. Dad and Betty live in Hernando, a couple of hours from Orlando. By the time Dylan and I arrived, we were both travel worn and ready to go to bed. Refreshed the next morning, we visited with Poppa and Betty and then set out to have an adventure. This isn't always what Dylan wants to do.

Dylan really enjoys just staying home. Getting him to agree to go sightseeing usually takes some work on my part to convince him we're going. Such was the case on this trip. I wanted to take him to see the manatees at the game reserve, but I knew he'd be just as happy swimming, reading or playing his Game Boy.

He reluctantly went, and we both had a good time. We watched the manatees underwater as we listened to an informative presentation on them; we held snakes and went to the alligator and hippopotamus pits for lectures. All that was fun and interesting, but it was the drive home we can't get out of our heads to this day. I took a wrong turn and ended up on an alternate route that was more like a ride

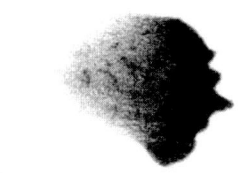
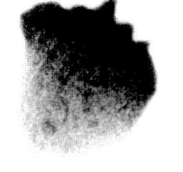
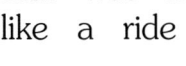

through
the countryside
than a trip on the main
highway. As always, Dylan
was riding in the backseat, and we
were talking about the day and commenting on the different homes along the

way. Then, as I looked up ahead, I saw something in the road. At first I thought it was a dead animal, but then it seemed to move. I kept driving; and as I began to swing out of the way, another car approached. I had to swing back. Splat! As the car bounced back down, I realized I'd run over a turtle—

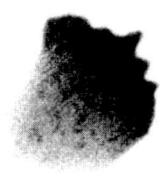

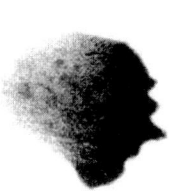

a very large, hard-shelled turtle. I felt absolutely terrible.

Dylan couldn't get over it. He kept talking about it and talking about it. All the while, I felt sick about what I'd done. There must have been a way to prevent it. What if it was someone's pet? It was so big. I should have slowed down. It made such a loud cracking noise. Why didn't I see it sooner?

For both Dylan and me, that accident is more firmly implanted in our memories than the manatees are. I hope when you take special trips with your grandkids you have many treasured memories—and very few turtles crossing your path!

PAT B.

Newport Beach, California

our of our grandchildren live relatively close, and the other is somewhat farther away; he's just turning three. Last Christmas, his parents—our daughter and our son-in-law—gave us a little webcam, so on Sunday evenings we often have a Web chat with our grandson and then with his parents. We read him a goodnight story with the webcam. We hold the books up, and we choose the one to read. It's a great way to bridge the distance.

We have a little home on Cape Cod, so the whole gang is up there in summer and we spend lots of time out on the Cape Cod flats. We started going to Cape Cod when my younger daughter, who is the mother of four of our grandchildren, was 11 months old and her sister was four years old. Cape Cod was a mainstay in their lives, and it has become that now for the grandchildren. The children really want to be there as badly as their parents, and even our sons-in-law want to be there, so that's another way we handle the separations.

JANET C.
Princeton Junction, New Jersey

ver the Fourth of July, when Caylin was four, we flew from Houston to Chicago, where we rented a car at the airport. Then we drove to Indiana to my mother's house. Caylin was thrilled to be staying with her "greatest" grandmother.

That trip will go down in family history as one of the highlights of all our lives. My brother, Ed, had a family reunion at his lake house in Michigan, where we enjoyed boating, swimming, fishing and our favorite family pastime: eating. Both my brothers have all daughters, and the girl cousins were excited to be part of Caylin's first trip away from home. We sang and danced and watched fireworks and stayed up far too late. No one wanted to miss a second of our time together.

Twice during that trip we drove into Chicago, a fascinating experience for a four-year-old; but it was also Caylin's first time in a very large Northern city. The tall buildings, the noises, the museums and yachts awed her, just as I had hoped they would. She saw "trains in the air" and took a "taxi-Cat" ride. We went to the American Girl store, which was more fun for my sister, Nancy, and me than it was for Caylin, who has probably been jaded by overblown toy stores in Texas. During our six days together, not once did Caylin complain about anything. She was never cranky or complaining and chose to fall instantly asleep in her car seat when Nancy and I were driving between destinations; or she played happily on the floor at my mother's house accompanied by my sister's dog, Max, and surrounded by the same Tinker toys and Lincoln Logs I had played with when I was a child.

I wondered at Caylin's ability to live in the moment, to enjoy only what is at hand without the adult mind-set that "living means worrying"—about tomorrow, about bills, health issues and an unending list of concerns. Caylin's outlook was what we all wish to attain in our meditations and prayers: This was her bliss.

As we flew back to Texas and I watched Caylin looking out the airplane window, I took the chance to voice the one great fear I'd had on our trip: "What are you thinking, Caylin? Do you miss Mommy and Daddy?"

She looked at me with eyes so penetrating that for a nanosecond, I could see Caylin as the woman she would become.

"I do. But I miss Great Gramma already. I miss Aunt Nan. I miss Max." Then she held my hand. "When we go home, I'm gonna miss you."

I was stunned. "But I live in Houston, honey. We aren't that far away from each other."

"But you don't live in my house, Gramma."

My heart shredded.

"No, I don't. And I wish I did."

"Me, too."

We spent the rest of the trip holding each other, holding hands, and reciting to each other the memories we had just made so we would never forget them.

Oddly, even at the time, I sensed a change spreading over my life. Something was about to happen, though I didn't fully integrate it into my thinking right then. What was interesting to me was that Caylin, only four years old, had perceived exactly the same thing. This fragment of time would soon become more than just a fun trip. It would be a golden memory. I was about to move away.

Within six months, my career turned on a dime. I had started what I thought was a small film company in Texas. Though I had been writing novels and nonfiction for 20 years and had been delving into screenplay and teleplay writing for more than 15 years, I had not, up to that point, really pushed the envelope.

Unfortunately, for that side of myself who would like to become the grandmother of my own dreams for Caylin and play with Barbie dolls and help her to ride her two-wheeler without training wheels, the other side of myself, the career side, made the choice this time to push the envelope—at Mach speed.

In order to establish my company properly and be taken seriously, I had to face the fact that I had to relocate to Los Angeles.

Emotionally, I made it through the sale of my beloved home to lovely strangers; but let's face it, I'd never even met the buyers before signing the closing papers. I had the usual concerns and fears I've always had when I've sold a house I've poured my heart into. Will they actually talk to the plants like I did? Will they spin enough dreams in the rooms? Will they remember to put out the flag on every holiday, including Christmas? Will they know that the unhappy woman who walks past my house every day is dying? Will they know the names of everyone's dogs the way I do and remember to pet them under their chins like I did?

I made all kinds of promises to Caylin about coming back. I even showed her the plane tickets for a return trip. But we both knew the truth. We do not live in the same house; and whatever we make of our lives, it will never be enough. Never enough time together, never enough I love you's, never enough hugs. I still hold dreams of taking Caylin to Paris and finding out what she will make of the foreign language I endeavor at times to teach her in spoonfuls. I wonder if she will cherish art and its makers as much as I.

So, Caylin and I will do what other grandmothers and granddaughters do. We will write to each other, talk on the phone, send emails and goofy computer cards, exchange presents on holidays and see each other when time and money permit. We will grow older but continue to love each other. We will do the best we can with the time we have been given.

CATHERINE L.
Scottsdale, Arizona

t h e n

Propellers. 28 passengers.
New York to Chicago
non-stop.

asey and Paula's new baby was born this past August, and since they lived about five miles down the street from us in Las Vegas, we were babysitting or visiting two or three times a week. Sometimes we kept the baby on the weekends so they could have time to themselves.

They always came to us. We had promised ourselves—and them—that we would never be overbearing grandparents who push ourselves into their orbit all the time. What turned out to be funny was how they came to us because we were not forcing ourselves into their lives. They'd call and ask us: "Do you want to go out for a bite to eat? Or we can bring a couple steaks over and throw them on the grill." They loved being with us. We'd watch movies together, and they'd bring over DVDs we all enjoyed.

Then my son had an amazing job opportunity open up in California, and it just broke our hearts. We had a lot of heartache dealing with the idea of them moving away. But the good news was that although Casey had also been offered a job in New York City, even farther away, the one in California was a better job. So he and Paula and our two grandchildren are only five hours away now instead of 2,000 miles from us.

To every cloud there's a silver lining. We still visit

quite a bit, but the situation has changed dramatically. For three years Donovan had been part of our lives every single day and was calling us on the phone and sending us emails. From the time he could speak, he would point to the front door and say, "Nonny, Poppy, Nonny, Poppy." He always wanted to be with us, just as we wanted to be with him.

In dealing with the geographical issues, we have technology to thank. We're a very computer-literate family, from the youngest to the oldest. Donovan himself, at the age of about 15 months, was sitting at the computer and rolling the mouse around. By two years old, he had learned to click on the icons Casey set up for him, and he could open up Bob the Builder and Barney the Dinosaur. Casey also put in an Internet camera, so we have Internet cameras on both ends—at our house and at his house.

Whenever Donovan wants to see Nonny and Poppy, he just clicks on the computer and clicks on the camera. His parents will usually tell us what time this is going to happen, so we make sure we're home, and we talk to each other by video camera. Then at least once a month we hop on our motorcycle and we take a nice trip over to Irvine, California, and spend the weekend with them. And once a month they hop in their car and they come the opposite way to spend a weekend with us in Las Vegas. We're seeing each other at least twice a month, and we also have the Internet connection with video cameras so we can stay in touch between visits.

Donovan also calls us on our cell phones. We have one voicemail message from him that we've kept for more than a year now. It starts out with, "Nonny, Poppy"—and then he starts to tell us something—

and then his dad takes the phone away and says, "Okay, now, Mom, Dad, I want to ask you a favor. Would you do this or pick this up or drop that off . . ." and we hear Donovan's little voice in the background go, "Hey, I was talking to Nonny and Poppy." And then as my son continues to leave a message, Donovan gets more and more agitated in the background. Finally, he's yelling, "I want to talk to Nonny and Poppy!" so they put him back on the phone. This is a little boy who's usually very calm and quiet. This is a hilarious phone message, and we play it whenever we need to hear his voice.

JEANNE C.
Las Vegas, Nevada

NOW

Jet engines. 500 passengers.
New York to Singapore
non-stop.

y daughter's husband had a wonderful business opportunity to move to Portland. We were all very excited for them and for the kids. They were going to live in Oregon, which is such a beautiful place. But the pain of being separated was so enormous that, on the day they left, I don't know who was crying harder, the grandkids or me. I had promised myself that I was going to be strong and encourage the grandkids to be excited about this new adventure of moving, but when they threw themselves on me and cried so uncontrollably, I couldn't stop. It was an agonizing moment for all of us. I had bought them really cute, very cuddly stuffed rabbits that were kind of funky and weird and fun.

After we calmed down a bit, I explained to little Katie, who was crying the hardest, that Grandma had put her heart in this rabbit. Katie could take this rabbit with her and hold her and hug her and always know that Grandma's heart was with her. That seemed to help her. But to this day, as you can probably tell, I

get choked up just thinking about it.

SUZAN Ĥ.
Las Vegas, Nevada

y daughter and her husband live in Northern California, and I live in Southern California. I've visited them just about every month since the grandchildren were born, and they spend a week here every summer. Whenever they need me to baby-sit, I just drop everything and go.

Even before they had children, I used to go up every couple of months to visit. My daughter and I are very close. She's my only child. And when my grandchildren were born, I said to her and my son-in-law, "Whether you want me or not, I'm going to be up here once a month. They're not growing up without me."

Coming from a very close Italian family, my daughter wouldn't have it any other way, because her grandparents were very important to her.

LORRAINE T.
Fullerton, California

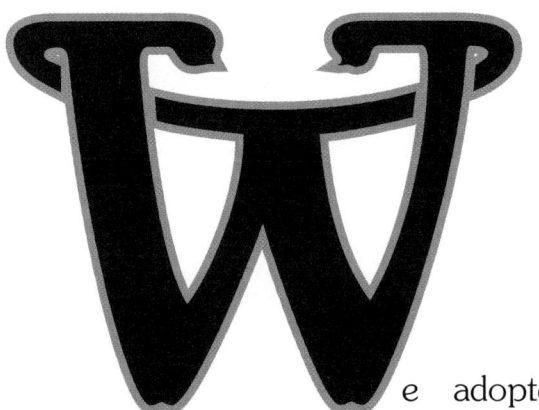

We adopted our daughter Ginger when she was three years old. I will always remember one day some years later when she and I were cleaning a mirror in our house. As she looked at her reflection in the mirror, Ginger asked me something about how she had looked when she was a tiny baby. I said, "I might not be the best person to ask about that, because you didn't come into our family until you were three years old. I'm you're mother, but you weren't actually born to me." Then Ginger said, "Well, I wasn't born to you. But I was born for you." What a wonderful, unforgettable thing to say!

I feel like all our children and grandchildren were born for us. I just wish we could see them as often as we wish we could. In the past, there was always so much going on. I had been divorced, and then I went back to school and eventually got my PhD and started my career as a psychologist. The value I placed on the kids was always there, but putting that value into action was hard. Now that situation has changed, or even reversed. Our first priority is to be with our children and our grandchildren, but they aren't always able to do that. So we try to see them as often as we can and to make the most of every moment.

SONJA P.
Oceanside, California

There is a common thread of emotions spun through these stories concerning distance: Living far apart really is easier said than done. The ideas from these long-distance grandparents and the guidelines that follow can help us deal with the challenges of a world in which our families are no longer right around the corner.

GRANDPARENT GUIDELINES

✳ As quickly as possible after they're born, hold your new grandbabies; whisper your love to them in their ears

✳ Designate an item that they instantly know represents you

✳ Put something in the mail often; even if it's just a card, make it lumpy and bumpy

✳ Discover their best time for a weekly telephone call, and call consistently

✳ Schedule trips and excursions together

✳ Visit www.grandparentsrock.com to learn more about vmail (not the same as email!)

NOTES

Grandparents
ROCK

45
RP

PURPLE PEOPLE EATERS

**Without heroes, we are all plain people
and don't know how far we can go**

Bernard Malamud

CHAPTER 4

PURPLE PEOPLE EATERS

A happy childhood is one of the best gifts grandparents can help give their grandchildren. Grandparents Rock is made up of stories, and this chapter is about the gift of telling stories to your grandchildren. Often, the sillier the stories, the better they are. I love to tell stories, and my grandchildren love to hear them. In fact, I believe they even need to hear them. They need to know that the funny thoughts running through their heads are shared by at least some of the adults in their lives. That's the importance of silly stories. And that's the profound purpose of "Purple People Eaters." (Try saying that three times fast!)

I learned from some very good storytellers myself. I was the oldest daughter of five children, and my parents didn't have time to sit and read to me. My grandfather was exiled in Canada until I was in the fifth grade, and my grandmother wasn't the read-to-me-in-bed type. At age 11, I was given the charge of caring for my siblings, as my mother was diagnosed with multiple sclerosis. I helped my father get everyone off to school in the morning, and after-school care was my responsibility too. Playing outdoors was my reward of choice. There was no time for reading. If I had any free time, I wanted to be out and about—away from my duties at home and from my brother and sisters.

Growing up with my very outspoken Croatian grandmother—we shared a room when I was in high school—I really learned the art of telling stories, not just reading them. My grandmother had grown up in the former Yugoslavia before coming to America as a young woman. She still spoke with a thick accent, and her spellbinding stories of war and strife captivated me. She spoke seven languages, had beautiful light gray eyes, attracted many male admirers and was a true psychic. My grandfather was a handsome, distinguished, displaced Yugoslavian nobleman from a long lineage of royal blood. After coming to America, he made a living as a gardener while working on becoming a millionaire (which is a different story, full of intrigue, glamour and corruption). Both of them were fascinating, mysterious and truly creative. Some kids might have found them a tiny bit scary, but not me!

Although I might never match my grandmother for narrative talent, I do my best. Conversations and storytelling with my grandchildren have a special place in my heart. Dylan, for instance, is not a big talker. Until Dylan was 12, he was basically an only child. He learned to entertain himself to a great extent. But since you can only carry on conversations with yourself for so long, he appreciates it when I get the ball rolling. Spending time with Dylan has taught me a secret about connecting with more-reserved children: first, tell them a story about you. I like to tell about something I saw or learned since we were last together. Afterward, I'll ask Dylan what he thought about my story. I begin with specific questions like "What?" "How?" "When?" and "Where?" This keeps the conversation moving. But vague questions like "Why?" invite equally vague replies, like "I don't know" or "Just because." For me, one purpose of thinking up a story is to learn what my grandchild is thinking. And it works. Dylan often shares his inner self with me, sometimes to the surprise of his mother. A safe and loving environment can be created by your words and the sound of your voice. This chapter is full of ways for creating a space of close trust and imaginative fun.

Bedtime stories are a very important part of our family rituals. We've always done this with our kids, and now my son Casey has carried on the tradition. He always puts Donovan to sleep with a story, and his favorite book has always been one of my favorites too. It's called The Mini Bug and Other Silly Creatures, and for the longest time that was the only book he wanted to hear at bedtime. He wanted to know about the Mini Bug and little Barb Schnarb and all these other crazy creatures. And sometimes I will just make up stories for him. Usually I put him in the story, which he always likes. The only problem with that is, when he's in the story he doesn't want to go to sleep. He wants to hear how it ends!

I have a head full of crazy stories, and that's how I make these things up. Donovan knows me as Nanny, his grandma, but he also knows me as the Story Genie. He knows that Nanny is a little wacky.

I have a thousand people living in my head, and they all come out to play when I'm entertaining kids and especially when I'm entertaining Donovan. We do voices, accents, characters and silly sounds and sound effects. I used to do a lot of voice-over work, so I've got a whole repertoire of people in my head—everything from Irish to English to Spanish to Italian. I use a lot of dialect in my storytelling.

JEANNE C.
Las Vegas, Nevada

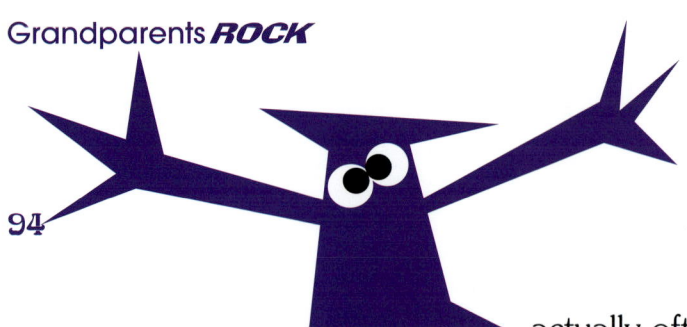

actually often tell my grand-kids stories that my mother told me about China. My mother was in China with my father and sister for four or five years in the late 1940s and early 1950s. She has a wealth of fabulous stories. My grandson is fascinated by one story about people with elephantiasis—he's fascinated by the idea that you could be twice your natural size. He actually thinks that's good, you know?—that it's really cool.

MECHELE F.
New York, New York

e do a lot of reading in our family, but we also make up stories. We've often done that at nighttime, and we let the child take the lead into the next part of the story. We try to make the child the subject or hero of the story. But I've found that we are really a big book-reading family, and I think we enjoy that probably more than anything: all the children's classics, from Good Night, Moon to other wonderful things.

JANET C.
Princeton Junction, New Jersey:

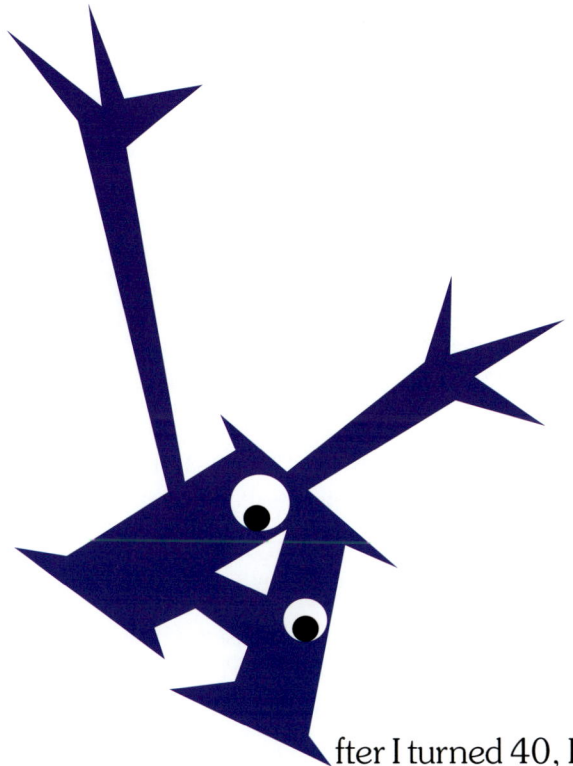

fter I turned 40, I needed glasses. Often I'll have the book but I won't have my glasses, so I just read the story by looking at the pictures and talking about what's happening. Of course, my grandson is used to the story the way his parents read it. He'll say, "But Ya-Ya, that's not what the words say. Where did you get that from?" I just make it up as I go along, and he thinks it's really neat.

HEIDI W.
San Clemente, California

hen I begin a story, I have no idea how it will end. My stories twist into a new direction at every turn. If I become lost as to where to go next, I'll have the main characters go off for some meditation and thought or to listen quietly for some sound that directs them. It's most important to have fun with the story. The better ones usually don't make much sense. The end is always perfect and comes at exactly the right place because no one has heard the story before this very moment.

Sometimes Dylan is tired and will struggle to stay

then

Squirt gun. Get wet.

awake. I'll ask him if I should stop, and he'll always say no. I'll continue for a short while and then tell him it's "to be continued tomorrow" and that I love him. He nods his head and drifts off to sleep telling me he loves me too.

The next night he's eager for the continuation and end of the story. Even though Dylan was drifting off to sleep the night before, the content he is able to recall amazes me. Kids' minds are like sponges. However, "Part Two" is not my preferred choice of delivery. Even if I've continued the story only twice, I find it more difficult to finish the third night. I lose my momentum. After two unsuccessful attempts at "to be continued," I now finish the story quickly when I see he's not going to make it until the end.

PAT B.
Newport Beach, California

W e have an agreement that I'm going to tell them a bedtime story and then they're going to tell me a story. Usually we use magazines. You look through the magazine and you find a picture that you like, and then you make up a story about that picture. That's how we really tell bedtime stories. But there is one true story I have told many times. It's about a journey I went on when I was studying Native American culture, a journey with a couple of shamans. We went out into nature for about 10 days, for what is called a "dream walk." I have many times told my granddaughters the story of the dream walk, and to this day they always want to hear that story.

SUZAN H.
Las Vegas, Nevada

What I really love about the end of the day when I'm telling the story is the cuddling and the little giggles when I do a funny voice. I'm changing my voice and acting to make the clouds and the flowers talk. It's like the clouds and flowers or whatever's in the stories are talking to the babies.

The little four-year old loves anything with Sesame Street. He's got oodles of books and he wants me to read them all. I think it's to delay bedtime. The twins love What Tickles You; the book has actual fur on the little animals. Moo-Moo, Brown Cow is a favorite, and they thoroughly enjoy How Many Hearts because the hearts are really shiny on each picture.

JANE M.
Azusa, California

NOW

Water blaster. Get drenched.

y mother read to us every night, maybe because she was a schoolteacher. My favorite story was called Bunny Blue. I don't know why that was my favorite, but it was. Somehow my sister found a copy of it, and I read it to the grandkids. They also love movies, so sometimes we watch movies instead of read. I've got a queen-sized bed, but my bedroom's very small. We prop a bunch of pillows against the wall and the bed is big enough so we can all climb in under the down comforter and watch movies together. That's our togetherness.

SYDNEY B.
Tulsa, Oklahoma

n talking about my grandchildren, I often use the word cherish. But that's a word I never used until I had grandkids. It never would have crossed my mind before—just too sappy. But now I use it about my grandchildren and about my wife too. I even think words like Grandpa and Grandma should be cherished. For kids, there will always be love and safety in those words. No matter what.

RICK M.
Oceanside, California

Most of my made-up stories begin with "Once . . . upon . . . a . . . time," delivered with drama, timing and a deepened cadence. It's not just the words but also the delivery that makes made-up stories unforgettable. Once he hears those four little words, Dylan wiggles underneath his covers, settling in for a peek into my mind. Pink poodles (standard size) that run the world; ducks that are blue on one side and green on the other with magical powers; a brilliant child, whose head was a single eye and who hid for seven years in the forest; trees that talk; being lost and surviving on a desert island; underwater worlds; aliens that are seeking the mystery of making perfect chocolate cookies; a brave little boy or girl; angels; and secret languages are just a few of my story topics and made-up characters. So put away your glasses, prop up a pillow and let the purple people eaters in your imagination run wild!

If you'd like to hear one of my stories, I have a couple of them on my Web site: www.grandparentsrock.com. It's an MP3 file, and downloading is easy.

GRANDPARENT GUIDELINES

* Read to your grandchildren

* Be famous for something in your grandchild's eyes

* Made-up stories never have to make sense and can be continued later

* Outrageous and unbelievable characters are always the best

NOTES

Grandparents
ROCK

45
RPM

Ninety-Six Tears

Sure, I'm for helping the elderly.

I'm going to be old myself someday.

Lillian Carter, in her '80s

CHAPTER 5

Ninety-Six Tears

As a grandparent, you may feel like a kid again—but you also know that you're not. You're ready to do whatever your grandchild feels like doing, but you also know you can't always do it. The real trick is to have the most fun you can within your limits, and that's the focus of this chapter.

If I could have one wish for my physical self, it would be for complete wellness and physical ability. Sometimes I watch toddlers stumbling and tumbling. They pop right up and start over again. It looks so easy. They don't have too far to fall, of course, and they're light enough so the impact is minimal. But things change. By the time you're five, a fall while running or riding a bicycle can mean a painfully skinned knee. By the time you're 55, falling might not mean just a boo-boo anymore, whether you were riding a bike or not.

I have some mobility restrictions, and I deal with them. They're not horrific, but they can be depressing in the moment. They limit me in what I'm able to do with my grandson, Dylan. I know I'm not alone. As we continue on our path of maturation, there are more stiff joints, backaches and knee challenges than when we were in our 30s or 40s. My own physical challenge advanced my body age by 20 years practically overnight, and it's all due to a medical overdose.

After a prolonged business trip to Vietnam

in 1998, I was completely overtaken
with pain and near delirium from an
illness involving my liver. With medication
my liver healed, but I was kept on the
medication three and a half months longer
than recommended, and I was left with
excruciating pain in my feet. I couldn't
walk, drive or even shower because
water on my feet was too painful. I was
diagnosed with peripheral neuropathy
from an overdose of Flagyl. This changed
my life forever. No more dancing, hiking
or even walking for long distances. After
18 months of medication and treatment, I
improved. During all this time I was working
for an advertising agency. They had me
traveling and speaking to real estate
groups all around the county. I would take
my walker to get around as best I could.

Fortunately, I had many wonderful friends
who stood by me. They supported me with
love, care and much, much more. More
times than I care to admit, I went to bed
crawling on my hands and knees crying
in pain; and there were times on airplanes
when I would shout in pain as the nerves
would try to reconnect and miss. If it hadn't
been for my friends and family, I would
have spun out of control with depression.

It's been almost six years since my
neuropathy began, and I have improved
greatly; however I must monitor the
amount of time I am on my feet.

I learned a great deal from this experience. There are many people, maybe millions, who live with constant pain. I recognize their faces. Sitting at a traffic light, I'll watch someone slowly cross the street and I'll know if their feet hurt. While shopping one day, I saw a woman gripping her cart and trying to make a purchasing choice and I could see pain on her face. It wasn't pain like "Oh, which one should I buy?" It was more like "Why am I here?" Until you live with pain 24/7, you may not ever notice it on another person's face; but once you do, you are forever changed and you instantly recognize it in others.

A year ago my grandson, Dylan, and I decided to hike up a hill at Picacho Peak in Arizona. I wasn't able to go as far as he wanted, and I had to stop many times to rest my feet. Sweetly, he asked me how long I would be handicapped. I told him I was so much better now, but that I thought this was as good as I would ever be. Children have such compassion. He said he was sorry and he would stay with me and not to worry about how far we climbed.

What's the point of all this? Encourage your grandchildren to experience all that they can. Play sports, be active, and test your limits for as long as you can. Don't sit it out. And by all means, grandparents, if you're physically able to ski, or dance or hike . . . GO FOR IT! I am a healthy person.

If I had received the correct amount of medication, I would be as active today as 20 years ago. I do my best to focus and be grateful for what I am able to do now, because I know there certainly could be something ahead, something to set me back, something which I won't even have a clue about or see coming. It's the game of living—enjoy every minute.

What if you have a disability? What if your grandchild has a disability? We learn to adjust. We learn to appreciate what we are able to do, without ever giving up or giving in. There is still a lot of living to do whether it's from a wheelchair or with a walker or cane. Some of my best times with Dylan have been just playing a game at the kitchen table or making up wild bedtime stories. Your time together doesn't have to be physical. Looking back on my life, I'm really happy I danced, roller-skated, surfed, skied, went camping, white water rafting and hiking, ran in races, played sports and simply enjoyed the physical abilities that God gave me. I'm truly glad I did all that, and I want to keep doing it. The abilities may be different, but the intention is the same.

 few weeks ago I slipped when I was getting something out of my car, and I slightly sprained both my wrists. They were black and blue and swollen. My granddaughter wanted me to pick her up, and she didn't understand when I told her I had boo-boos. When she needed to go upstairs. I couldn't lift her like she was used to. In order for her to not cry about going up the stairs—because she's only 21 months old—I told her we were climbing a mountain. I would crawl up the stairs and she would go up with me. Then, on the second day my daughter wrapped my arms and both my wrists in Ace bandages, and my granddaughter finally understood that Ya-Ya had boo-boos.

If I take them to the beach, I'm thinking, "Okay, I've got to pack an ice chest with food, I've got to pack a diaper bag, I need this and this and this. I've got one kid walking, but he may not walk all the way to where we're going in the sand. Then I've got this other one who doesn't walk at all, and I'm limited on the amount of weight I can carry. How am I going to strategize to get all this stuff to the beach?"

Those situations can be a real challenge. I have osteoporosis, so sometimes it can be hard just holding my grandkids in a certain way. But even if you have a stiff neck and a sore arm and you're home alone with them, you've got to deal with it. Either take an Aleve or just grin and bear it.

ḤEIDI W.
San Clemente, California

onovan has been blessed with an angelic childhood so far. God willing, it'll continue. He hasn't seen anything traumatic or of a difficult nature that we would have to explain to him. The most difficult thing we've had to explain so far is where the cat went. We had an elderly cat named Poochie that passed away due to age, and it was hard for Donovan to understand where Poochie went. We had to explain that Poochie was no longer with us and that Poochie had gone to kitty heaven. Now, whether that's the wisest thing to tell him, I don't know. But I do know it's a little easier for the child to accept if he believes that a beloved pet has gone somewhere happy.

JEANNE C.
Las Vegas, Nevada

 was in Santa Barbara, living with a boyfriend. It was fine as long as my kids were married and childless, but once grand-kids came along, it changed the relationship between the two of us. The relationship was breaking down to the point where, when my grandson was three months old, my boyfriend asked me to move out. I didn't have a place to go; I didn't have funds saved because I really wasn't expecting it. I found myself in a situation where I was in a home renting a room and I had to put all my things in storage. Here's my grandson on the way, and I'm renting a room. I didn't have a home for him to come to and spend time with me. I couldn't drive down and pick him up and bring him to my home because I didn't have a home.

Even today, I don't have a home. I relocated, and I live in a house; but I only rent one floor of the house. I don't really have a place for the kids to come spend the night with me. That's been a real challenge, and I have a lot of guilt about that. I don't have a home where I put down roots because I'm still kind of grow-ing up myself.

I live at the beach at San Clemente, so my grand-son says, "Ya-Ya lives at the beach. I want to come to Ya-Ya's beach." When he talks about coming over to my house, he relates it to the Pacific Ocean and the beach and surfing. That's kind of unique; but for me it's also hard, because I don't have a home where he can come and bake cookies with me. Probably the hardest challenge in the four and a half years of having a grandchild is not having a secure living environment for myself and for him. But it works, as I said, because he doesn't know any different. I think it's also a great memory to have, because if something were to happen to me, he would think that my home was the Pacific Ocean and the beach; and the ocean and the beach will always be there.

113

HEIDI W.
San Clemente, California

few weeks ago our granddaughter called me. She's just becoming a teenager. She was crying because she and her mother were having a little conflict, and I realized that it was the first time this has happened. She was telling me about the problems she was having with her mother, and I said, "Well, maybe it's that both of you are starting to deal with the changes that are happening to you. Maybe it's about something bigger than just your homework." But she kept crying and crying. Finally I said, "Now just take some deep breaths.

then

Glass bottles with paper caps.

Breathe in. Breathe out. Breathe in. Breathe out."
And finally she started to calm down.

The next day, my daughter called and said, "I need
115
to thank you for helping my daughter get through a
hard time." But the important thing was my granddaughter was the one who said to her mother, "I
guess you know I called Gaga." I wasn't the one who
told her mother about the call. If I had been the one,
my granddaughter would have felt that I had betrayed
her trust.

SYDNEY B.
Tulsa, Oklahoma

y daugh-
ter in Florida had a stillbirth at approximately seven
months. I actually consider myself a grandmother of
six, because I held that stillborn boy in my arms and
sang to him and rocked him before releasing him.
We all were present during the stillbirth; we had a
memorial service for him on a beach. I remember
that my other daughter's children were all anticipat-
ing the arrival of their first cousin. They got the news
of what had happened, and they didn't quite know
what it meant.

Even so, they seemed to accept the fact that this had happened and we were going to go on from that point. I think children are always a little bit more accepting and understanding than grownups are about things that are closer to heaven.

JANET C.
Princeton Junction, New Jersey

When my granddaughter was six or seven, I was taking care of her for a weekend while her parents were away. She went over to the house of one of her friends for a play date. It so happened that this was a family that was not well known to her, and my daughter had suggested that I make a call about one hour into the play date to make sure everything was going okay. When I called, from what I could hear it seemed like there was something not right over there—apparently a boy was sort of beating up on his sister. When my granddaughter sounded odd on the phone, I said,

"Okay, I'm going ask you some questions that just need yes or no. The first question, are you having fun?" She said, "No." "Do you want to come home?" "Yes." "Do you know what to do?" "No."

Then I said to her, "Now we're going to have something new just between you and me, and it's called a white lie. I want you to tell the mom that there's been a change of plans, and that's why I called. I have to come by and get you early. Can you do that?" She said she could, so I went and got her. What happened that afternoon was a tremendous bonding experience for us. She's 12 now, and even to this day she says, "Grandma, remember when you told me what a white lie was?"

MECHELE F.
New York, New York

n o w

Paper cartons with plastic caps.

ometimes my back can act up a little bit—maybe after a hard day cleaning house or whatever. Little kids don't always understand when grandparents hurt, so I explain it that it's like when you fall down, how it hurts right there for me. If my grandson still wants to play or he still wants to swing or something, I explain to him how it hurts there and I let him suggest to me what I can do to make it feel better but still be part of what's going on. I can watch him swing, or we can go play cards, or we can shift the games to things where Grandma can kind of take it easy.

JANE M.
Azusa, California

 y grandson had just turned five. He was born eight weeks premature. Of course, we were not prepared for that, and I was very concerned. I remember holding my daughter's hand really tight when they brought the baby over. What happened was so amazing, because she had always been talking to the baby while she was pregnant. When she spoke his name, he moved his foot toward his mama's voice. I was thrilled that I could be there to witness that; it was something very dear.

At the age of eight months, he had to have a surgery done on a heart valve. It was about four days before Christmas, and I went to Chicago to give my daughter and my grandchildren a sense of comfort and support. He had the surgery, and he came through just fine. We had been feeling very stressed about it, and I'm so grateful we were able to be together during that time.

PAT C.
Newport Beach, California

 would say that the biggest unexpected challenges I've had with my grandchildren are concerned with discipline. Compared to my granddaughter, my grandson is a very picky eater. The kids' parents were away for the weekend, so we were taking care of them at their house for three days. We barbecued some steaks outside and made this really fun dinner, but when it came time to eat, we sat down for this nice meal but my grandson wouldn't eat any of his food. It had been a really fun three days, and within a 45-minute period it became all whining and crying.

I sent him to his room while his sister was finishing dinner, and he had a complete meltdown. He just cried and cried and wanted me to come upstairs. My daughter and son-in-law came home about an hour later, and they were a little bit peeved at me because they felt that the discipline was too strict for his age. He's four and a half, and they just thought that it was too strict to send him to his room when he wouldn't sit at the table and eat. Although that's the discipline they used in their home, when I used it they were not happy about it. It disturbed me enough to the point that I actually wanted to go home and leave it all behind.

As a grandparent, you feel like you have a certain prerogative to discipline the children in your care, but then in reality your boundaries are dictated by the parents, by your grown kids. It's not about the wisdom you feel you've gained in raising your own children. You can't use that same discipline on your grandchildren because you tend to step on your adult children's toes. That was a lesson I learned.

ḤEIDI W.
San Clemente, California

Children are like sponges.

They soak up everything. Grandparents with disabilities, including myself, have the privilege of implanting permanent impressions of compassion. These lessons have the capability of sticking like paw prints in wet cement.

I have to admit that the refrain of "Cry...cry...cry...cry" running through "96 Tears" (one of my favorite '60s songs) now reminds me of the challenges of aging instead of running to the dance floor on a Friday night at the crowded Tustin Youth Center. But there's never any point in being a crybaby, regardless of your age, right? Just keep dancing as long as you can!

GRANDPARENT GUIDELINES

✳ Take good care of yourself

✳ Stay as active as possible for as long as you can

✳ Encourage your grandchildren to get out and play

✳ Disabilities don't have to mean distance from your grandchildren

✳ With whatever limitation you may have, there are lessons to be gained

✳ You can teach patience, tolerance and compassion

NOTES

124

Grandparents
ROCK

45
RP

*Bye Bye
Love*

**Holding anger is like grasping a hot coal
with the intent of throwing it at someone else;
you are the one who gets burned**

Buddhist proverb

CHAPTER 6

Bye Bye Love

In the Introduction, I spoke about the ability of classic rock songs to evoke powerful emotions. "Bye Bye Love," in my opinion, is certainly one of those songs, but for me the emotions are no longer about getting asked to the prom. This chapter tackles the complexities and challenges that families—including grandparents and grandchildren—must face in today's world. Sometimes we just have to make the best of hard situations, but learning to do that is an important lesson at any age. And showing how to do it is certainly one of the most valuable gifts that a grandparent can give.

> *Bye bye, love.*
> *Bye bye, sweet caress.*
> *Hello, emptiness.*
> *I feel like I could die.*

I had such an emotional connection with that song! Separations of all kinds are a big part of being a teenager— separation from your own childhood self, for one thing. For that matter, letting go has been a part of my adult life, too. With two divorces under my belt, I know firsthand that breaking up is hard to do.

It's not easy to be candid about these matters, but since many contributors to Grandparents Rock have frankly shared the "left turns" their lives have taken, let me do the same. My first marriage, to Mike Burns, lasted long enough to produce two beautiful daughters, and it set me on my path of self-reliance. I'll always be grateful that I had my family when I was young.

In the early '70s, the women's movement was in its early stages. The message of burning your bra and getting ahead in the corporate world was not affecting the young women I knew. It wasn't so unusual to be starting a family in your early 20s, as I did.

It was 1971, and I was attending Chapman University. To pay my student loan, I worked as a hostess at a popular businessmen's restaurant, and that's where I met Mike Burns. After we dated for a mere three weeks, he asked me to marry him! We had a small family wedding; and 18 months later, I gave birth to our first daughter, Michelle; Jennifer was born 22 months after that. And about a year later, we were getting a divorce. Bye-bye, love, indeed.

It seems to me that the '70s produced

more than its share of broken marriages. The decade certainly fell far short in living up to the idealized images of loving marriages and intact families we boomers had grown up watching on TV. Donna Reed, Leave It to Beaver and Father Knows Best may have been what we expected; what we got was Kramer vs. Kramer.

Recently I met a gentleman who had raised his family in a very exotic location. It wasn't Europe or Africa, however; in fact, it was right in the middle of Los Angeles. But it was definitely a very special environment: the former home of Ozzie and Harriet Nelson. It was the supremely tasteful dwelling in which Ricky, David, Ozzie and Harriet had actually lived and which also had been the setting for their television show.

My new friend shared some laughs about taking his kids through real-life adolescence in what had been a televised domestic Garden of Eden. But if anyone could ever believe that Ozzie and Harriet was an expression of how things really are, it probably wasn't Ozzie and Harriet themselves—and it certainly isn't anyone living in our contemporary world. We may want to shed a tear about it, but the iconic family life of the Eisenhower years has gone the way of the 17-inch screens that beamed it at us. In today's world, the stresses that couples feel are right out in front for everyone to see, including their children. When those stresses take couples past the breaking point, there's a very important role for grandparents in providing reassurance. Even where there has not been a divorce or a separation, the complex relationships and configurations in families today call for the stabilizing influence of grandparents.

Sherlock Holmes referred to Dr. Watson as "the one fixed point in a changing universe." As a grandparent in the 21st century, you may not have to be quite that stabilizing; but as the contributors to this chapter show, there's definitely work to do.

y daughter and her husband were separated for a month while she was pregnant with her second baby. They say the mother's emotional state is very important to the baby; and my daughter and her husband were having some trouble, so she and her first child, a little boy, came to live with us for a month. I was worried because my husband and I both knew what it was like to go through a separation and divorce. What is gained is not much; what is lost is a lot. Your heart just breaks for them as a family, and you know there's not a darn thing you can do about it.

At the end of 30 days, they called the marriage counselor who had recommended the separation, to set up an appointment. The receptionist said, "Oh, I'm sorry, the doctor isn't taking any appointments. He's going through some personal problems." My daughter and son-in-law got back together, and now they have a "marriageable" marriage. That should be a new word, I've decided. How's your marriage? Marriageable.

SYDNEY B.
Tulsa, Oklahoma

y grand-children call me Ya-Ya. I'm sure other kids know their grandmothers by many different names. After all, there are all kinds of families today. When I found out I was going to be a grandparent, my ex-husband had already remarried and a question came up about what his wife would want to be called. She just wanted to be called by her name; she didn't want to pick any kind of name that suggested the identity of grandmother, since she didn't want that role with these kids.

She is 11 years younger than my ex-husband, and at that time she had a daughter who was seven years old. It's quite complicated for him. He's dealing with being a father and a grandfather at the same time. This makes the role of grandparent for him a lot different from mine.

HEIDI W.
San Clemente, California

I recognize that, with my stepchildren, I'm not going to be the traditional, biological grandmother—so I take the role of the "Auntie Mame" grandmother. Both my stepchildren have come to love me, but they don't quite look at me as a maternal force. I think they look at me as a very wise, business-savvy mentor, because their moms are not in business the way I am. As grandparents, both the biological grandmothers are wonderful cooks, wonderful storytellers, all that sort of thing. They know the whole family history up and down. I am more the Auntie Mame type. I'm the one who knows the city. I'm the one who knows how to do stuff. I'm the one who writes with them sometimes, because that's what I do for a living. But the important thing is that all the grandparents like each other

then

The ultimate family car.
Gasoline cost 25¢ a gallon.
(Ethyl was a nickel more.)

and respect each other. Even after divorces or whatever, this family is your family for the rest of your life,
even the part that you divorced.

MECHELE F.
New York, New York

ylan had been vis-
iting my parents' home since his birth and was comfortable there. During the time I was staying there,
my dad gave me the master bedroom to use, and he
even gave me space in the garage to park my car.
However, in spite of his generosity, I knew it wasn't
my home and I had to respect that.

Dylan would stay for long visits. I wanted him to
enjoy our time together. I had always had a great
place to live; and even though now I didn't have my
own house, it was important to me to create happy
memories with my grandson. I told him bedtime stories, cooked for him and played with him there. The
backyard had a large, beautiful pool, and Dylan loved
to swim. I like to think having Dylan and me in the
house helped my dad through his mourning process
after the death of my mom.

During the time I lived with my dad I was traveling back and forth to Vietnam for my work. While I was out of the country, my father fell in love with Betty Lou, a woman from Florida. Three weeks after my final Vietnam trip, I was hospitalized after a near-death experience. While I was still recovering and very weak, Betty Lou helped Dad sell our big family home, and off they went to build a new life. I had to find a place to live immediately and move more things into another storage center.

I had been diagnosed with peripheral neuropathy. Fortunately, I was finally under the care of a good and kind doctor. Slowly I began to heal, and with the help of a walker I began to travel and speak to real estate groups for the marketing company. But sometimes the pain was indescribable. Dylan was living in Tucson and, fortunately, didn't see me often during this time.

For a time I stayed with my friend Connie and her family, but I needed to find my own space. I was traveling more and more and was earning a better income, but I was still paying off huge credit card debt accumulated from months of not working and from the loss of my speaking business. Luckily, I was introduced to Aurelia.

Aurelia and her husband, Lloyd, owned a nice big home in Mission Viejo and had a downstairs bedroom and bath that they offered to me. Lloyd was a traveling project manager and had an apartment in Texas. He would come home every other weekend. Aurelia was happy to have my part-time company, and I was happy to have my own downstairs room.

While I was living with Aurelia, Jennifer and Dylan moved to Mission Viejo and found a place to live only three miles from me. This was a wonderful time for

Dylan and me. I bought him his first Harry Potter book and he would come and spend the night with me when his mom worked the graveyard shift at the hospital.

One thing I'm known for in my family is my love for comfortable beds and buttery soft sheets. When Dylan visited and crawled into bed with me, we would squirm and giggle joyously; and within minutes we were both sound asleep. Aurelia was kind to us both. She would enjoy with us Dylan's adventures hunting roly-poly bugs and butterflies in her backyard gardens, and she made us both feel very much at home. But once again it was not my house.

Fast-forward a few years: I'm back in California, no longer with Aurelia, after a six-month business trip to Bangkok. I'd been uncertain of my career, living in hotels, staying with friends and sometimes family. I finally land in a wonderful three-bedroom condo with a magical patio and a big tree in the front yard. I remove everything from storage and once again make a home of my own.

I have painted the living room, entry and dining walls Ralph Lauren red, the office a soft purple and the guest room yellow. My treasured antiques are put

n o w

The ultimate family car. Gasoline costs $2.50 a gallon and you have to pump it yourself.

in place, and I've bought a new living room sofa and a plush, new pillow-top bed. Yes, at last, this is my home.

Now when Dylan comes to visit me, I know the meaning of "let it be," and I have a place where I can allow it to be. I have a single-seat hammock hanging on my patio that Dylan calls "the womb." (His mom is a certified midwife, and from a very early age Dylan has been comfortable with hearing about the birthing process.) As soon as Dylan arrives at my home, you can find him swinging in the hammock either reading or playing his Game Boy. I call out and ask him where he is, and he'll shout back to me, "I'm in the womb." He and I love our time together.

During one of my visits to his house, I was unpacking my suitcase and he was keeping me company, visiting with me along with his dog, Buddy. This is our usual routine. His mom came in the room to check on us, and Dylan enthusiastically told his mom that the room already started to smell like Gram! I was so startled and immediately began to worry that I had that "old person" smell of too much perfume (or of mentholatum, which I don't even use). I had to go deeper on this one, no matter what the outcome. I asked Dylan if it stunk. He told me it smelled good, "Like you, Grammy." Whew! I'm glad I asked.

PAT B.
Newport Beach, California

e have been through all kinds of family rearranging and restructuring. I tried very hard to maintain a relationship with my daughter's ex-husband for the sake of Katie, so that she didn't feel she was being pulled in different directions. He was a very good father. Then he got a job opportunity in Portland, an enormous opportunity. His pay scale more than tripled. No one in their right mind could pass this up. He absolutely had to take the job, but it meant Katie had to live with either her mom or her dad. And even though her dad is a wonderful father, her mom felt that she could provide better for her, because a daughter needs a mom. She just felt it was best for Katie to be with her. Her ex-husband, of course, was very distraught at the idea of losing his daughter. Even though she tried to make provisions to fly Katie for visits on a regular basis, he still felt a need to fight for custody of Katie. I admire him for that decision, for caring so much about his daughter that he wanted to keep her permanently in his life. Unfortunately, when it got to a court battle, it got ugly. Many false allegations were made against my daughter that were clearly unfounded and untrue. It definitely caused a division between my former son-in law and me.

At that point, I decided that I needed to just love Katie through all this and not show any bias. I also needed to stand by my daughter, so I didn't attempt to keep up any further communication with her ex-husband. Had he reached out to me, I would have been there for him, but he didn't. It was probably just as well that he didn't, because my daughter needed me to be on her side and support her. Fortunately, the judge ruled that Katie would stay with her mother; and then after that, things settled down.

SUZAN H.
Las Vegas, Nevada

For me, there has always been great comfort in the belief that everything happens for a reason, even when it means saying bye-bye, love. Divorces are almost always painful, but often each person learns more about life and love. Good grandparenting expands the presence of forgiveness and love, which are most needed during times of family strife and separations.

GRANDPARENT GUIDELINES

✻ Your relationship with both of your grandchild's parents brings enormous comfort to your grandchild

✻ Keep the drama of your children's relationship ending out of your life

✻ Radical forgiveness is the key to a happier, healthier life and the most important lesson you can teach your grandchild

✻ Center yourself as the purest example of love and forgiveness

NOTES

142

Grandparents
ROCK

45
RP

HAPPY
TOGETHER

It's not what you gather,

but what you scatter

that tells what kind of life you have lived.

Helen Walton

CHAPTER 7
HAPPY TOGETHER

144

Singing is something I particularly love to do, so this chapter about making music with your grandkids is one of my favorites. When Dylan and I drive together, the car is our Carnegie Hall on wheels. Dylan listens to me sing, and I hear him ever so faintly singing along too. At a stoplight, we're the people you see in the car next to you singing with all the windows up—all you see is our heads bobbing and our lips moving. You look over and you can't help but stare. Then you smile and wonder: what song are they singing, anyway? (Hint: "Happy Together" is our all-time favorite.)

We also love to "harmonize" with the CD or the radio. In particular, we enjoy oldies stations and kids' stations like Radio Disney. But it's no longer just a matter of turning on the radio and starting to snap your fingers. Call me an ol' grandma, but the harsh percussion and brutal lyrics of some of today's music are like a punch to the solar plexus. It's hard for me to imagine that people really like listening to this stuff, and it's absolutely impossible to imagine singing it with my grandchildren! On the other hand, I don't deny the talent of many rap musicians. We all just have to trust our intuition—and I know what I like.

I do like Prince, for example, I've played his Purple Rain tape in the car when my grandchildren were along. I knew when and where "certain words" were coming along, and at that point there would be a mysterious, temporary interruption of the tape. The kids and I also like the Beach Boys, the Beatles, the Turtles and the Supremes, along with other groups that avoid topics of hate and violence.

Maybe it was growing up in the '50s and '60s that made me something of a creative spirit, although it didn't start out that way. Drinking and drugs were not part of my experience growing up in Southern California. My father was a retired Marine Lt. Colonel fighter pilot, and my mother was also quite strict. For me, as a teen, sex was completely out of the question. Once, after a date with the best-looking guy in my senior class, I stood at the front door with great anticipation of a sweet good night kiss. Just as he leaned in to kiss me, my dad opened the door and authoritatively said it was time to come in. How embarrassing! It didn't take long for the story to circulate around the locker room and strike fear into the heart of nearly every guy I dated thereafter.

I wasn't exactly a square, however. I went on lots of dates, attended plenty of parties and had a blast in high school. Later on, in college, I did experiment with marijuana, sex, peace marches and demonstrations—I lived a modified version of the Swingin' '60s. But the biggest part of my youth experience in the '50s and '60s was my love affair with music. Watching American Bandstand, learning the Mashed Potato, the Monster Mash, the Twist and plain ol' jumping to the music formed the core of my daily life then, along with babysitting, talking on the telephone, homework, cooking family dinners and helping to raise my four siblings. Today, as a grandmother, I can reconnect with those meaningful moments by sharing music with my grandchildren. It's being happy together in a truly magical way.

usic is a very big part of the fun my grandson and I have together. One of the things that really makes Donovan giggle is when I take songs he recognizes and then insert his name. He really enjoys being the star of the song. The old cartoon Spiderman had a theme song: "Spiderman, Spiderman, does whatever a spider can." We do "Donoman, Donoman, does whatever a Donoman can." And he just thinks that's hilarious. We use everything from the Spiderman theme to old standards, as well as Beatles songs. Donovan was introduced to rock 'n' roll and that era of music from the time he was just a few weeks old, when I would rock him to sleep by dancing around the family room listening to the Bee Gees and Sergeant Pepper.

I was always a theatrical kid. When I was three years old, my mother put me out on stage at a centennial celebration in South Jersey, dressed as a little Davy Crockett. I had to sing, "Davy, Davy Crockett, king of the wild frontier," and I had to do the whole song! Well, I got out there, got a few bars out, and a lady in the very first row started laughing. Now, as I think back, she was laughing a kind of "Oh, isn't she cute" laugh. But when I was three years old, it was very traumatic.

All of a sudden, I stopped singing and started crying; and they had to drag me offstage because I was weeping my little heart out. But even so, from that point on I was always involved in music. I was always involved in school plays, doing choir at church, singing Christmas carols throughout the neighborhood with all the carolers. Music was a big part of my life when I was little, and it is an important part of what I do and who I am today. I passed that connection to music along to my kids, and they have passed it along to Donovan as well.

When Donovan was very tiny, maybe nine months old, he was in the car seat in the backseat and we were playing this fun CD from a group called Ugly Duckling. They had this one particular song that had an awesome beat to it. Dan, my husband, looked up in the rearview mirror and he said, "Look at Donovan." So, I look back at him, and he's got the head going around in a circle in time to the music. He's doing this little jive move in the car seat and he's got the chin going around, the head going around in these little circles, in perfect time to the music. We knew then that he was a music lover.

JEANNE C.
Las Vegas, Nevada

t h e n

Drum set requires dextrous use of arms and legs.

J'm from Char-
lotte, North Carolina. We had a black radio station
called WGIB, and it would play all the Motown hits
and all the music by African-American artists coming
out of Memphis and the South. You couldn't hear a
lot of that music on the so-called white stations or
the pop radio stations, but you could hear some of it.
But then, on the black radio stations, you could never
hear the Beatles or the other incredible music that
was coming out that I loved. I had to find it on the
pop stations. I was never a big rocker, but I liked Cre-
dence Clearwater. I liked all the music that I heard on
the radio, but I didn't call it rock 'n' roll. I just called it
music. It would have been "Come See about Me" by
the Supremes, "Bernadette" by the Four Tops, "Red
Rubber Ball," the Moody Blues, the Byrds. I just used
to love the sound of it all. But I didn't really quite get
Jimmy Hendrix until after Jimmy had died. I grew up
leaning more toward R&B.

In the late '60s, there was a real strong pop feeling
in African-American music. You had Curtis Mayfield
and the Impressions and James Brown—it was just
exploding and it was all original and fantastic. That
kind of musical orientation and experience spoiled
me. I was used to good music, so I wasn't ready for
the music I hear today. It just leaves me cold, so I

don't listen to the radio much anymore. . . .

My granddaughter Jada loves the "Morning Chant," which is a song that I wrote. At the choir rehearsal she sings it, and she claps her hands and dances. She dresses like the choir dresses, and she lines her dolls up and conducts her own choir. She's got a great voice, great pitch, and all four of her grandparents are musicians. At church, when I'm conducting the choir, sometimes she stands right there beside me conducting too!

RICKIE B. B.
Los Angeles, California

love to dance. The radio is always on K Earth, an oldies channel, and we're dancing constantly. Sometimes my little grandson will come up to me and say, "Grandpa changed our channel." A lot of times, if there's a good song on, I'll go over and crank up the volume. Then we're all dancing, even my pet bird. He's really into music, too.

One time, "Brown-Eyed Girl" was playing. That's Grandma's favorite song. "Pretty Woman" is also good, because you can really dance to that one.

And we can have a lot of fun with "These Boots Are Made for Walking," by Nancy Sinatra. But this time, "Brown-Eyed Girl" was cranked up high, and we're all dancing, even the bird. I remember looking at the bird and the babies, and I'm thinking, "They all dance alike!"

Another time when we were at a birthday party there was a DJ playing music from the '60s. Tommy was only three at the time, but he recognized the music. Only a few people were out dancing already, and a bunch of us ladies were all sitting together. I tell you, no prom queen or new bride ever had the feeling that I had when that little three-year old walked over to me and said, "Grandma, will you dance with me?" And he took me out on the dance floor. We had cameras flashing, and it was a moment that I will never, ever forget.

JANE M.
Azusa, California

n o w

Drum machine requires dextrous use of fingers.

ur granddaughter, who is eight, went through a wonderful Dixie Chicks spell, and we would sing along with the Dixie Chicks in the car. With the younger children, anytime they're in the car with me, we put on Peter, Paul and Mommy, which is one of our favorite collections of songs for kids, done by the Peter, Paul and Mary group. There's another one that they love—"The Boa Constrictor"—"I'm being eaten by a boa constrictor, who's at my toe. . . ." Once, we were in slow, heavy traffic, so we took the "Boa Constrictor" song and had fun turning it into "I'm Stuck in Traffic on I-97."

I also enjoy dancing with my grandchildren. I can remember being in a grocery store with my older grandson when he was about five, and some wonderful rock 'n' roll music came on. We just stopped in the middle of the aisle and started boogying together. I guess that's another thing you can do when you're a grandparent and you're not 16 anymore. You have no self-confidence issues. Music was always an important part of my life. I loved music and I loved dancing. And now I'm a five-time "Grammy" winner. It's really the best award anybody can receive.

JANET C.
Princeton Junction, New Jersey

e're a family of singers, and we sing all the time. None of us can sing worth a hoot, but we are definitely singers! The very first song that I taught them—and they all know it—is "Oh, What a Beautiful Morning. Oh, What a Beautiful Day." And actually, that's the first song that my parrot learned as well. We always enjoy singing that song, but we have graduated now to a new favorite song, written by Randy Newman for A Bug's Life, called "A Certain Time of Your Life." We've been singing that song for about six years now, and the grandkids perform it. I also have a very large collection of percussion instruments. Anytime I'm at a garage sale and I see bongos or maracas or tambourines, I'm always picking that stuff up. I have baskets and baskets of percussion instruments!

I have had the good fortune of enjoying a career in the jazz community, and a lot of my friends are very famous jazz musicians. They often come to visit us. My grandkids have had the privilege of sitting in during drumming circles and playing with some of the greatest musicians in the United States. Drumming is a really big deal for us, as well as singing. I have all kinds of music that I've collected from all over the world, and when my friends and my grandkids come over, we turn on the drumming music really loud. We

ACROSS

1 Liquer

6 TV Show

7 Men's accessory

8 TV device

9 Kitchen appliance

10 Hairstyle

11 Carpet

13 Short-lived craze

15 Lava _____

17 A Clockwork _____

HOW MUCH CAN YOU TELL YOUR GRANDKIDS ABOUT THE DISCO ERA?

(HOW MUCH DO YOU WANT TO FORGET ABOUT THE DISCO ERA?)

DOWN

2 _____ ball

3 Gold accessory

4 _____ spirit

5 Saturday Night _____

7 Type of shoes

12 Big _____ (where disco began)

14 Disco queen

15 Plant

Solution:

See last pages of book, and go to

www.grandparentsrock.com

for more puzzles, trivia and fun!

Have your grandkids
ever heard of a
**CROSSWORD
PUZZLE**
?

get out all the baskets of percussion instruments and go at it.

I happen to believe that music is a heavenly language and that it's one of the ways that God communicates with us. I think that's why people respond so well to music. If you look back through history, even to very primitive tribal times, people have always found a way to create music. Rhythm and tone resonate within the human soul. But now there's something different going on. I actually have a very deep fear of some of the music today that's delivering scary, violent messages. I really do miss the hippie days when we sang about peace and love and the message was stop worrying and join together and let it be. I really think that spirit needs to be re-infused into our music.

SUZAN Ƕ.
Las Vegas, Nevada

Early prototype for the walkman.

 remember when the twins were born, I spent the first three weeks after they came home from the hospital helping my daughter. I think I drove my son-in-law crazy because I found a dusty radio out in the garage, wiped it off and brought it in. I got the oldies station, and the babies just loved it. One baby would be crying after eating, and the other one would be sleeping. I would take the crying one, and we'd listen to music. That was so soothing. I also noticed how, when I'd be trying to get them to eat and they were just not having any part of it, music would really help. I'd be dancing and acting silly; and then, without their knowing it because their eyes were on me, I'm popping in extra bites. In the meantime, I'm getting a workout. It's like killing two birds with one stone!

JANE W.
Azusa, California

It's great to know I'm not alone when it comes to the importance of music in the lives of those of the rock-n- roll generation. There are so many ways in which music expands our lives, our being and our souls. Whether it's the sound of a bird singing, an instrumental piece heard at a concert, a love song, a happy melody or the rhythm of a grandchild's heartbeat, music fills the heart when words fail. It's the universal language that bonds all cultures and nations.

I like to introduce my grandson, Dylan, to music from around the world. We'll listen to music from India, China, Africa and anywhere else we can find. I hope you're doing the same with your own grandkids. After all, we're the generation of soul. Let's keep the music rockin' in our grandchildren's lives.

GRANDPARENT GUIDELINES

✳ No matter what kind of voice you have, sing with your grandchild

✳ Lock in a favorite song with a grandchild and you'll have it forever as a bond

✳ Expand your music collection. Go to Barnes & Noble or Borders and discover new CDs at their listening stations

✳ Try making up new words that personalize characteristics of your grandchild through favorite old songs

✳ Take your grandchild to a concert in the park to hear live music

NOTES

160

Grandparents
ROCK

45
RPM

LET IT BE

The weak can never forgive.

Forgiveness is the attribute of the strong.

Mohandas Gandhi

CHAPTER 8

LET IT BE

One of the most wonderful, and useful, tools in a grandparent's bag of tricks is a pure, almost Zen-like acceptance of the way things are in the moment. As you'll see in this final chapter, there are often huge benefits to "letting it be." It may be that only the older persons in a family understand the importance of this, because until we've repeatedly seen that most things really do work themselves out, we can't really keep a sense of perspective. By the time we become grandparents, chances are we've learned something about going with the flow.

Even if we can't teach everything we've learned to the rest of our families, we can certainly exemplify it in our relationships with those we love. We can "speak words of wisdom" and act upon them too.

Kids today live in a world of high expectations. In fact, studies have found that of all the things a contemporary parent hopes for, including winning the lottery, nothing is more to be desired than a high-achieving child. The flip side: Nothing is more daunting than raising children in the modern world. In this environment, a lot of things can go wrong; and on any given day literally everything can seem to go wrong. Help is definitely needed—and as these contributions show, grandparents are a perfect resource for providing that help.

Every summer my grandson visits from New York and stays with us for at least two weeks. We enjoy that time with him; but on one of his visits, we discovered that he was playing with neighbor kids and coming home with all these new toys. When I asked him where he got these things, he would tell me that he had bought them from the neighbor kids. Of course, I needed to go over and talk to the parents to make sure they were aware of the transactions and were okay with them.

I assumed that he had come from New York with his own savings; but in talking to his mom, I discovered that he didn't bring any money with him. Then we had to start uncovering where the money was coming from—and of course it was coming from sneaking into Grandma's purse or Grandpa's wallet. We had to have some very long talks about why it's important not to do things in life that are not honorable, why it's wrong to take things you haven't earned, and what the consequences are spiritually when you make decisions that harm others. We had to talk a lot about the sin of omission and how not telling somebody that you have done something is the same thing as not being truthful. It was hard to go through that experience with him.

SUZAN H.
Las Vegas, Nevada

We've had our grand-children stay over at our house since right after they were born. Every Friday night and every Saturday night. First there was one child, then two; and when there were three, three children came. And we've never had a baby bed in the house, ever. They've always slept in my bed.

I don't work myself to death cleaning up every minute because I'd rather clean it up once, when they're all gone. I always tell myself, "This can be cleaned up, but it doesn't have to happen now." We have children's drawers. We have two, three, four of them in the living room, and you can just pull them out. All the coloring books are there, and their crayons, and when the visit is over you can just pick them up and put them back. Keeping everything really neat has never been an issue. That's one reason kids love to come over here. I don't let them play baseball in the living room, but if something is not going to hurt them or anything in the house, there's no problem. The only thing that they are absolutely forbidden to do when they are over here is argue and fight.

A really important time for us was when Jay, my husband, was in the hospital for four months waiting for a heart transplant. At the very last minute, when Jay had only hours to live, a heart showed up! Now he's had the transplant for 10 years. At the time this happened, we had three grandchildren. Quinn, the oldest, was three at the time. So there was a three-year-old, a two-year-old and a one-year-old. They'd all go up to the hospital, but Quinn is the only one who really remembers it. He hated to ride on the elevator, but he'd go up and see Papa in the hospital.

They even visited in their Halloween costumes, so Papa could see them. Quinn was dressed up like Batman, with all these muscles in his costume. He said, "Gwampa, I need to tell you something—can I tell you a secwet? These aren't my weal muscles!" Jay loved that. The grandkids' visits helped us all to keep going, and things were good. They knew, and they still know, how important life is and that it can go either way.

Five or six years ago, I was sitting on the back steps with my four-year-old granddaughter. We hadn't even been talking about it, but all of a sudden she asked, "Now, Gaga, Papa got his heart because . . . ?" She paused, and I said, "Well, a man named John was hit by a car, and he was going to die." I was trying to think what to say next, and this little four-year-old said, "Now I get it. John could give Papa his heart because he doesn't need his earth heart anymore because he has his angel heart." I told her, "You're right, sweetheart."

I still cry when I think about it.

SYDNEY B.
Tulsa, Oklahoma

My grandson always wonders whether I have a family when I go home. Do I have kids at my house? I tell him, "No, my kids are you and your mom and auntie." He'll say, "Do you have babies at home? "No, you and your sister are my babies."

Then he always wants to know where my mom and dad are, and I tell him they're in heaven. He wants to know what happened, so we talk about my parents' plane accident, and then he'll come over and say, "It's okay, Ya-Ya, they're angels. They watch over you, and they're up with God."

ĦEIDI W.
San Clemente, California

I've had little ones digging out all my pans and my Tupperware, and they're all over the kitchen and I could care less! Sometimes Tommy, who's four, gets angry or throws little fits, and he might toss something. I can always bring him out of it with laughter. I make a funny face or act like I'm looking at him; and then when he looks at me, I look away like I'm looking at the sky, and I'm whistling. Pretty soon, he's giggling about it. But then I have to talk to him and tell him how anger hurts him

Grandparents ROCK!

t h e n

Blackboards.

on the inside and how it can hurt other people, too.

One time Tommy was at the movies with us, and his Grandpa bought him a soda. With soda, you're going to have gas. And he burped really loud. I quickly covered his mouth; and I got real close to him and told him, "No, that's not very nice." Later, when we're on the way home, I give him a little lecture about how that wasn't very nice and he needs to remember his manners and that I was a little disappointed that he was acting like a little pig. It gets kind of quiet, and I hear this voice from the back. He goes, "But, Grandma, I am a little pig." I just cracked up. Oh, I didn't let him see me laughing, but I thought that was the funniest thing.

JANE M.
Azusa California

Ours is an interracial marriage, but we've found that children don't recognize that they're anything but children, regardless of what color they might be. When all of our grandchildren are together, they just play and love each other and have a really great time; it's a very heartwarming experience. We ourselves have had some adjustment to go through as an interracial couple. But what we discovered in our relationship was that my kids— once they got over the shock, or surprise, if you will, of the idea that I was marrying someone who's African American—and they got to know him, they just fell madly in love with him. My kids just think Frank hung the moon and the stars. It's like he's at the feet of God and gets all the direct communication. They absolutely seek his wisdom and his support and his friendship; they love him very much.

Two of his three kids have had a little more difficult time accepting the racial differences between us. But I think that's largely because over the last 20 or 30 years there have been more and more interracial marriages. It seems to me that some African-American women are uncomfortable about this and feel as though they're losing their men. I can understand this. I truly have great empathy for what they've experienced and for the pain that this perception might cause for them. But I think that that has driven some of the discomfort that has been present in our relationship with Frank's kids. I just trust and know that the more we all grow to know and love each other, the more we'll be able to see each other as people and see the contents and not the container. It was the contents that Frank and I have that caused us to fall in love with one another. It had nothing to do with our containers.

SUZAN H.
Las Vegas, Nevada

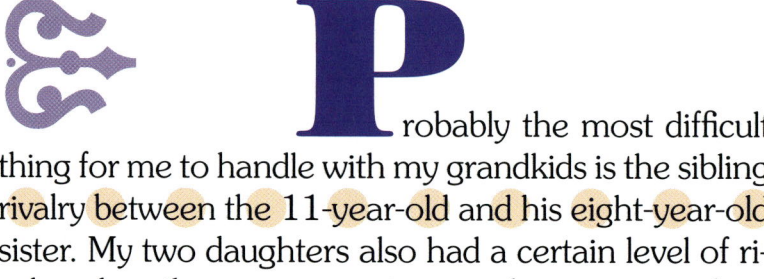

robably the most difficult thing for me to handle with my grandkids is the sibling rivalry between the 11-year-old and his eight-year-old sister. My two daughters also had a certain level of rivalry when they were growing up; they are very close now, so I always try to remember that people who have disagreements can still become close friends. But when I'm with my grandchildren and it seems like one of them is trying to work me into taking his or her side, that's when I have to step back and just let them work it out and not interfere. It's tempting to go in and break up the fight and say, "You've done this and you've done that"—but I just don't see it as the grandparent's role. I tried to intervene like that one time, and I felt very uncomfortable.

I made a decision that I would just take a breather when that kind of hostility came along. Sometimes that can be challenging, because I can see where one child may really have been slighted by the other. I have one brother who's 11 years older than I am, and we have always been devoted to each other; I don't have any personal experience with sibling rivalry to help me deal with this in my grandchildren. It's easier for me as a grandparent to just sit back and say, "Let me know when we can start talking to each other again, when we can come back together."

There's a fun story about our grandson learning to ride his two-wheeler when he was visiting us. Back home, he had seen some sidewalk sales, and

now

Whiteboards.

Grandparents ROCK!

he wanted to have a sidewalk sale to sell his training wheels. We could see that it was really important to him: He wanted to divest himself of something from his "old" life in order to move into a new life. We set up a little stand for him. But we actually didn't want to get rid of those training wheels, so, surreptitiously, we had a neighbor come over and buy the wheels for $2. Our grandson was thrilled. We still have those training wheels hidden away, and they will come out again someday—at his engagement party, perhaps. They'll show up at some point when he'll be happy to reconnect with another time in his life.

JANET C.

Princeton Junction, New Jersey

My oldest granddaughter, who has now turned 13, is very attractive, very flirtatious, very alive. She loves dancing, loves singing, loves the whole performance aspect of life. As her grandmother, I worry that she's going to end up making decisions that aren't going to be the best for her in the long run. I just have to trust that it's going to work out, but I certainly would make different decisions at my age from those I see kids making at their age. It's been difficult for me to find that fine balance between being Tesha's grandma and loving and supporting her and also being responsible to be the wiser one and offer advice that would be helpful for her.

One of the biggest challenges that I've had with her so far comes from the fact that she likes to confide in me. She feels she can talk to me about anything, for which I'm grateful. However, there have been many times that she's shared things with me that were actually alarming and that I felt her mother needed to know. But I also do not want to dishonor or break the confidence between us; it's an extremely fine line to walk. I haven't really figured out the right way to handle situations when she asks for my confidence and shares things that her mother should know. I know her mom would feel betrayed if she knew I had knowledge of some of the things Tesha's told me but didn't tell her. I've chosen to honor the confidence with my granddaughter and not share it with my daughter, but I'm not entirely sure that that's the right decision.

Here's one of the situations that occurred most recently. Tesha had been on a visit to her other grandma. She showed me that she had gotten a bellybutton ring, but she didn't want me to tell her mom. This wasn't exactly a life-threatening issue; but on the other hand, I was fairly certain her mom would want to know this—so I struggled with it. I really didn't want to disrupt the confidence that Tesha had in telling me what's going on in her life, because maybe at some time I'll be able to help her to avoid making a really bad decision. I really didn't know how to classify the bellybutton ring, but I was certain that her mom would want to know about it. I decided to wait it out to see if her mom would discover it on her own, and, thankfully, she did. But it was a bit of a crisis for me!

SUZAN Ɦ.
Las Vegas, Nevada

My dad passed away a year ago. He was 88 years old, and my daughter was very, very close to him. Matthew, who is five, knew my father better than his little sister, Rachel, did. When Dad passed away, of course we all went back to Pennsylvania for the funeral. Rachel didn't go to the service, but we felt that Matthew was old enough. But he kept wanting to know why None— Italian for "grandfather"—was in a box. We told him, "Well, that's what happens when you go to heaven." He said, "You mean he gets mailed to heaven?" So then we tried to explain it to him.

My father was a veteran. At the funeral a soldier presented me with a folded flag. I said to him, "I'd like you to present that to my grandson." The soldier went over to Matthew, who was sitting on his mother's lap, and stood in front of him. Matthew's eyes were like saucers. The soldier saluted Matthew and handed him the flag. Matthew's hand was straight out like a board when he took the flag. He was so beside himself he didn't know what to do. After the

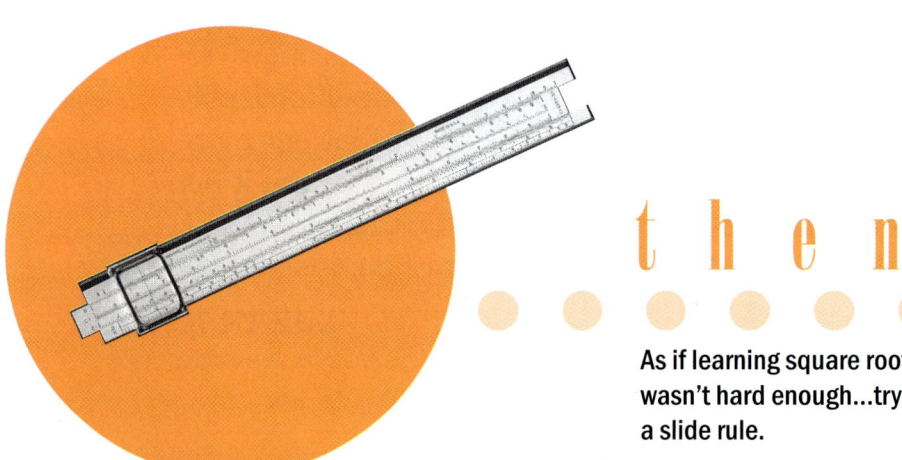

t h e n

As if learning square roots wasn't hard enough...try using a slide rule.

ceremony, he was still clutching the flag. He came running over to me and said, "Nonie, is this really mine?" I said, "Of course it's yours." And he said, "Nonie, we've got to put this in a frame and put it in my bedroom."

LORRAINE T.
Fullerton California

173

I think I'm much better as a grandfather than I was as a dad. I was busy making a living and making sure the kids behaved well. In those days, if you had noisy kids it meant you had a weak, undisciplined family. Now I'm down on the floor making noise right along with them.

The biggest surprise has been discovering my capacity to love. As a young father, I saw my family keep growing, and it seemed like there were just more and more coming. After number four, I really wondered whether I was going to be able to make this work. But now, every grandchild is just pure joy.

RICK M.
Oceanside, California

When I was a young child, my grandfather used to take me on a very special journey one day per year. Just he and I would head downtown and observe the world around us. If he happened to recognize a person of some importance, he would always introduce me, using a phrase like, "Excuse me, Mr. Mayor, I would like to introduce you to my grandson, Jay." Then I would be encouraged to shake their hands in greeting. Some conversation always followed. I learned who I was meeting and what was important to them—and they would find out who I was and what was important to me. The conversation was always gracious.

My grandfather would always say, "Jay, never be afraid to stick out your hand and introduce yourself. Tell people why you think they are important and thank them. And always remember, you're just as important as they are!"

We met a lot of people, my grandfather and I. We shook the hands of mayors, Members of Parliament, nurses, doctors, servicemen and women, the Cisco Kid and Pancho, prime ministers, Prince Philip and even the Queen. When my grandfather took my sisters and me to the National Press Club in Washington, D.C., we were introduced as special guests to his friends Governor Scranton of Pennsylvania and Senator Barry Goldwater. We were also treated to the premiere viewing of the first walk in space. What an experience for a young kid! As a teenager, I was able to use my grandfather's encouragement to introduce myself and shake hands with the Reverend Dr. Martin Luther King.

My grandfather has passed on, but I've been able to maintain the tradition that he began for me. I've been pleased to shake hands with hundreds of extremely worthwhile and important people, including my wife, Anne, and my business partner, Lee, largely because of my grandfather's very earnest yet simple encouragement.

Based on these very rewarding experiences, I like to ask people a simple but very revealing question: What was your most important handshake? Usually the response is silence at first, then introspection and finally a wonderful, positive outpouring of experiences. I have heard stories of how people shook hands to say hello and good-bye to their loved ones. I've heard about individuals meeting their future life partners and spouses. I've heard how business partners sealed

n o w

Einstein could have saved a lot of
time with a calculator like this.

a contract with handshakes, how community leaders met, how families interact, how charity was offered and accepted. I've heard how my close friend's handshake saved the life of his child on a fishing trip and how he and his son still use the same handshake to greet each other, to this day.

What was my own most important handshake? There actually have been five of them, each one of equal importance. These were the very first handshakes from each of my children and grandchildren at the time of their births. Now those are handshakes!

I can guarantee that those handshakes were a sight to behold. I happen to be a very large fellow with huge hands. My children—Josh, Ryan and Rachel; and my grandchildren, Luke and Gavin—reached out with their tiny hands to tightly grasp my little finger. My wondering eyes could see through their fingernails and skin, little blood vessels showing clearly. I could feel the heat and incredible energy in their tiny bodies. At the same instant, they seized upon the warmth, strength, security, fearlessness, hope and calm offered by my hand. In that first handshake, they are expressing all their curiosity and their unconditional love. They're telling me how important I am to them, and I'm telling them how important they are

to me. I offer all of my commitment, my love and my promise to them. And, of course, in that same handshake I honor the tradition and wisdom of my own grandfather, Dr. Jesse George "Pat" Paterson, from so long ago. Over the years, I take every opportunity I can to repeat that handshake with my children and grandchildren and to tell them about the person who first showed me how important a handshake can be.

JAY P.
Waterloo, Ontario, Canada

Whether it comes through prayer, meditation, dance or reading a good book, a sense of peace and tranquility is a necessary ingredient for a happy life. This doesn't mean you should endeavor to become a Zen master. It's really just a matter of relaxing. When you feel stressed, it can be helpful to think about how you've handled problems in the past. For example, try to remember what you were really worried about on this date two years ago. If you're like most people, you won't be able to make that recollection. What does that tell you? Two years from now—or probably even two days from now—you won't be able to remember what's bothering you now. Just put things in perspective:

Speaking words of wisdom, let it be.

GRANDPARENT GUIDELINES

✳ Your home will be turned upside down during your grandchildren's visits— count on it!

✳ You will put it back together

✳ Learn to lighten up and let it be

✳ Forgiveness is a lesson we should learn to perfect in ourselves and also to teach to our grandchildren as soon and as often as possible

✳ Read children's books on forgiveness to your grandchildren—often

NOTES

EPILOGUE

As this book reaches its final stages, I've just returned from an unforgettable adventure, and the memories from that trip are still so vivid I'd like to share them with you. In my role as executive director of a group of entrepreneurs called the Inner Circle, I have the enviable opportunity to travel with the group to exotic locations around the world. Most recently, we traveled to the African nations of Kenya and Tanzania, which were indeed beautiful and exotic; but they were truly inspiring as well, particularly in the context of this book.

I am very grateful to my daughter, Jennifer, for allowing Dylan to accompany me on our Africa trip. It's a very, very long journey with limited access to communication, and trusting me with her precious son meant so much to me. I had a feeling that this would be a life-changing experience—a journey to a continent many dream about but few actually see for themselves. As it turned out, our visit really was life changing for both Dylan and me, although in a different way from what I had expected.

The surprises started early in the trip. At one point during our 23-hour flight, Dylan and I looked out the window of our plane and saw an otherworldly terrain crisscrossed by glaciers: Greenland. Dylan was so excited. I didn't know how much he knew about Greenland, but just the name of the place seemed to hugely energize him. "Is that really Greenland?" he asked, while he got his camera. We talked about the mystery of this place. Then he looked at me and asked, "Gram, will you take me there too?"

At that moment, I realized how important it had been for me to bring Dylan on this trip—and why all of us grandparents should include our grandchildren in the adventures of our lives, whatever they may be. The more we do with our grandchildren, the more they'll want to do with us; and that will bring everyone much closer. It had already happened for Dylan and me, and we hadn't even gotten off the plane yet!

Africa was certainly everything we had looked forward to. There were daily wildlife safaris, and for the more determined members of the group there was an opportunity to climb Mount Kilimanjaro, the highest mountain on the continent. There were amazing hotel rooms, one of which could have been in the film Out of Africa, with creaking floors and four-poster beds draped with mosquito netting. Wonderful as those things were, however, the most memorable part of the trip did not involve giraffes, movie moments or mountain climbing.

The poverty of Africa is as stunning as its scenery. This was first apparent as we drove through Nairobi to our lodgings on the outskirts of the city. Everywhere you looked the poverty was overwhelming. Just passing by one such area on our very first day, in the comfort of our air-conditioned vans, stirred up feelings of helplessness within us all. The kids in our group, all of them teenagers, were totally silent. As the saying goes, you could have heard a pin drop. I don't know what these teens were thinking, but I'm sure they had never had those thoughts before.

The next day in Nairobi we visited the Abandoned Baby Center built by Feed the Children Foundation. This amazing charitable organization was created by Larry Jones, a former American minister seen many times on television raising funds for his organization and his wife lovely Francis. As we began our tour of the Center, we saw a child asleep in an infant car seat. Ordinarily there would have been nothing very disturbing about this—but this child was four years old and so malnourished that his size was that of a tiny baby. Seeing this little boy, our group's burly "macho man" safari guide, Christopher Law, actually burst into tears. It all seemed like a metaphor for Africa itself: a big, powerful man in one aspect, and a tiny, helpless child in another.

I know our visit to Abandoned Baby Center affected Dylan and the other kids in our group just as deeply as it did me.

We passed through the nursery and some classrooms, but it was the toddlers at the Foundation who really captivated everyone. Once Dylan started playing with these little children, he had no interest in anything else. He just wanted to be with the toddlers who had been abandoned by their mothers or fathers. I saw that what he wanted to give them was the very same thing I want to give him: total and unconditional love.

With that in mind, it's completely understandable that Dylan showed little interest in doing anything else on the tour. He wanted to stay there. To give that kind of love is the greatest experience a human being can have. For those of us who are grandparents, we have the best possible opportunity to give that love. If there's one thing I hope to share by writing this book, it's the importance of choosing to make the most of that precious opportunity.

With so many memories of our African experience—hot-air balloon rides across the massive savannah during the wildebeest migration, visiting a Masai village, learning some Swahili, being chased by monkeys, watching hippos, elephants, lions and giraffes all at very close range—there was a lot to recall about this once-in-a-lifetime adventure. Later, when I asked Dylan for his best memory of the trip, he answered instantly. "It was the Abandoned Baby Center," he said, "and someday I want to go back to Africa with my own family. I want to bring my own children to help these children."

I simply can't put into words how I felt in that moment, hearing Dylan's expression of compassion. My prayer is that you'll take to heart the firsthand wisdom offered in these grandparenting stories and then spark those very same feelings in your own grandchildren. Their adventures and experiences with you can bring a lifetime of memorable stories for generations to pass along about you as the most far-out, rockin' grandparent in the world! That is my wish for you.

ACKNOWLEDGMENTS

Writing my first book has been accomplished on the shoulders of some fabulous mentors and colleagues. Marshall Thurber taught me the process of defining the stories and unlocking creative juices. Marshall is a very special, brilliant and kind man who has influenced hundreds of thousands of people. I am blessed beyond words having him as my friend and mentor. Marshall, for all your help and especially with the vision . . . I thank you.

The knowledge of how to create my book as a series came from my longtime and close friend Mark Victor Hansen. Mark is the co-creator of the *Chicken Soup for the Soul*® book series (147 titles and 143 million copies sold—so far), and no one knows more about the world of books and marketing. Mark, for all your "thinking bigger" guidance and vision . . . I thank you.

Robert G. Allen has my gratitude for reading my book and sharing his insights for three and a half hours on a long, bumpy dirt road from Finch-Hatten's campsite in Kenya on the way to Tanzania. Robert has the distinction of having appeared five times on the *New York Times* best-seller list, and his genuine interest in the success of my book touched my heart and altered some of my direction. Robert, for your time, talent and direction . . . I thank you.

It is my pleasure to thank my friend and close collaborator Mitch Sisskind for his countless hours of listening and helping me. His time and talent with some of the interviews and writing is greatly appreciated. With my busy life, working, traveling and being a grandmother, this book would still be a project and not being shared with all the wonderful people reading this right now. Mitch, you rock! And many thanks to my three proofreaders: my sister, Cathy Grothus; Marinda Bean; and Christine Bettencourt. Thank you for correcting my grammar, changing my wild punctuation and letting me know you loved reading my book. After writing my book I thought I was finished until I was introduced to the enormously talented artist Chaz DeSimone. Chaz has a creativity and vision like none I have ever seen for book layout, font design and style. Chaz, for your vision, design, talent, patience and love . . . I thank you.

There are many, many friends who have helped on this journey of completing this book. I want them all to know how much I appreciate all their support and help whenever I called on them, no matter how many times. My friends, you all know who you are, and I hope you know how much you all mean to me. Janet and Chris Attwood are two of these friends that I also call angels. They were just ahead of me having just finished their book *The Passion Test*. Janet and Chris, for your fresh, hands-on experience, guidance and tender caring I cannot thank you enough.

I want to thank all the baby boomer grandparents I interviewed for this book. Hearing your openness and details of your personal experiences was an absolute joy. Even though not all of your stories were selected for this first book, I am hoping you'll have more contributions for one of the next, soon-to-be, *Grandparents Rock* series.

On the home front, I want to acknowledge and send truckloads of gratitude to my personal assistant, Georgianna Chapman. Her countless hours of support, watching over me, running errands and straightening my life while I was working, writing, mothering and grandmothering is nearly saintlike. Georgianna, you are the big sister I never had and a blessing from heaven. I am so grateful to my neighbors and dear friends Jim Wilson and his wife, Kimberley Bennett, who introduced us. They moved away, and I miss their dinners when I had no time to cook and their daily checking up on me. Jim and Kimberly . . . I thank you.

Last, and it bears saying, certainly not least . . . I want to thank my two beautiful daughters, Michelle and Jennifer Burns, for their love, support and belief in me. Through good times, bad times, family trips, countless phone calls, crying and laughing there is no greater joy and happiness. Michelle and Jennifer, you both mean everything to me. I love you.

STORY CONTRIBUTORS

Catherine Lanigan Paradise Valley, AZ
Catherine is a partner of a motion picture company.
www.mountainzenproductions.com
E-mail: cathlanigan@aol.com

Heidi Wascher San Clemente, CA
Heidi, an entrepreneur and Reiki practitioner, is
owner of Santa Barbara's Gentle Embrace, a body
therapy lotion company.
E-mail: skis2sb@yahoo.com

Jane Mussmann Azusa, CA
Jane, a quality-control supervisor in Azusa, CA, has
two terrific grandchildren.

Janet Netherton Churn Princeton Junction, NJ
Janet is blessed to have five outstanding grandchildren. She is a corporate training consultant in
written and oral communications, and a writing
and presentations advisor at Princeton University's
Woodrow Wilson School.
E-mail: Jchurn7@aol.com

Jay Paterson Waterloo, Ontario, Canada
Jay and Anne Paterson's number-one role in life
is to be the very best mentors they can be to each
other, to their family, their extended family and their
friends. "We must be creative, learn, share and lead
so that our family and other families can fulfill their
visions. If we are to enjoy life, and get a real blast
out of it, then we have to be a great 'Grandma and
Grandpa.'"
www.empoweredwealth.com. Direct link:
www.empoweredwealth.com/bios/bio_jpaterson.html

Jeanne "Genie" Corcoran Sarasota, FL
Jeanne—"Storygenie"—is a writer and creative
director for children's multimedia.
www.storygenie.com

Larry Kirshbaum New York, NY
Larry has been involved in publishing for nearly 40
years as an author, publisher and agent, and has
worked for Newsweek, Random House and Warner
Books. He and co-author Roger Rapoport wrote *Is
the Library Burning* (Random House, 1970). Larry
has retired from 10 years as CEO and chairman of
the Time-Warner Book Group to start a new career
as a literary agent and founder of LJK Literary Man-
agement, LLC.

Lee Brower Bountiful, UT
Lee resides in Layton, Utah, with his wife, Lori.
Together they have eight children and six grandchildren. Lee is actively involved as a founder or board
member of numerous charitable, community and
corporate organizations. He is founder and CEO
of Empowered Wealth, LLC, an international consulting firm headquartered in Bountiful, Utah, and
advises clients on how to protect and empower their
financial and other assets. Lee is also founder and
chairman of The Quadrant Living Experience, LLC,
an international association of specialists who coach
strategies to optimize true assets. Lee is co-author
of *Wealth Enhancement & Preservation*; and his
new book, *The Brower Quadrant*, is scheduled for
publication soon.

Lorraine Turissini Fullerton, CA
Lorraine recently retired from her position as office manager with the Teachers Association of Long Beach and now has more time to visit her grandchildren, who live in Northern California.

Lynn Marcus Morton Grove, IL
Lynn, a retired fifth-grade teacher, recently moved from Illinois to Michigan to be closer to the "cutest, smartest grandkids ever!"

Mechele Flaum New York, NY
Mechele, a thrilled grandparent of four fabulous grandkids, is president of Marketing Fire, a New York-based consumer trend strategy consultancy, whose clients are Fortune 500 and entrepreneur companies.
www.marketingfire.com

Murray "Trip" Wolbach, III Highland Park, IL
Trip has two fantastic children and two fantastic grandchildren. He is a senior vice president at Draper & Kramer, Inc., a real estate company based in Chicago.
E-mail: trip.wolbach@draperandkramer.com

Patricia Conlee-Fearnley Newport Beach, CA
Pat, who is the program manager for the National Marrow Donor Program, has 10 grandchildren.
www.marrow.org

Rhonda Barry Qu'Appelle, Saskatchewan, Canada
Known by her clients as the "Wizard of 'Ah's,' " Rhonda focuses on helping individuals and organizations to discover the best in themselves: their true soul. An internationally renowned author and

facilitator, Rhonda is helping our world to shift from scarcity-based independence to abundance-based interdependence. She is the author of *Pretend Birthdays and Other Memorable Moments*.
E-mail: soulgardener@sasktel.net

Richard Mars Oceanside, CA
Rick and his wife, Sonia, live in Oceanside and will be celebrating their 21st anniversary this year. They have seven children and nine grandchildren. Rick is a speaker, reverse mortgage consultant and entertainer, and he works primarily with seniors concerning their healthcare and financial well being. As a teenager in the early '60s, Rick played drums and played with various bands as a singer and studio musician and he had the opportunity to record a song that features one of the best-known drum solos in history, "Wipeout." He continues to enjoy entertaining and lends his celebrity influence in support of many charitable causes.

Rickie Byars Beckwith Los Angeles, CA
Rickie, the music and arts director of Agape International Spiritual Center in Culver City, CA, composes the music that constitutes the sound of Agape. She has two children, who are also artists, and one wonderful granddaughter. As wife and creative partner of Dr. Michael Bernard Beckwith, Rickie shares grandparenting privileges with Michael to five additional grandchildren.
www.rickiebyars.com and www.agapelive.com.
E-mail: rickiebb@agapelive.com

Dr. Sonia Powers Oceanside, CA
Sonia assists people and organizations in realizing their full potential through her business consulting and training company. She is also an internationally known professional speaker and a licensed psychologist with a private practice in Oceanside, CA. Dr. Powers hosted the weekly Dr. Sonia Powers television show and is currently working on her latest work, *Turn Barriers into Bridges*.
www.DrSoniaPowers.com and
www.TurnBarriersIntoBridges.com

Suzan Hudson Las Vegas, NV
Suzan is a real estate investor, "green building" developer, real estate investing trainer, and the founder of Have a Peaceful Heart Foundation.
www.enchantmentway.com

Sydney Brady Tulsa, OK
Sydney and her three daughters, Jadene, Shelly and Terri, invented TUBTINTS, a children's bath product. Sydney (Ga Ga) and her husband, Jay (Pa Pa), celebrate weekends with their five grandchildren.

IDEA CONTRIBUTORS

Special thanks to those whose recollection of lifestyles in the Boomer years, and how they've changed today, contributed to the "Then and Now" feature in this book:

Rickie Byers Beckwith
Genie Corcoran
Christine Crosby
Mary Ann Doyle
Dona Donato
Joe Gray
Cathy Grothus
Christopher Law
Roger Leib
Janet Florence McCormack
Jay and Anne Paterson
Guy Rowen
David Smith
Tom Williams

DREAMERS & DOERS

Where would we be without the fabulous inventions of the Baby Booner generation, those machines and toys and tools which spurned the technological miracles of today! We salute the companies whose products appear on these pages:

Airbus S.A.S.
Conagra, Jiffy Pop
Douglas Aircraft
Dodge, Durango
Gabby's, babymarketplace.com
greatmusicproductsonline.com
Hasbro, Hula Hoop, Super Soaker
Magic Hoop
Recoton
Roland, Boss
Rollerblade
seashells.com
Texas Instruments

(ANSWERS)
TO PUZZLE & QUIZ

NAME QUIZ:

All these names are popular for either sex.

CROSSWORD:

ACROSS

1 Liqueur: MIDORI

6 TV Show: CHIPS

7 Men's accessory: PURSE

8 TV device: VCR

9 Kitchen appliance: MICROWAVE

10 Hairstyle: FRO

11 Carpet: SHAG

13 Short-lived craze: FAD

15 Lava LAMP

17 A Clockwork ORANGE

DOWN

2 DISCO ball

3 Gold accessory: CHAINS

4 FREE spirit

5 Saturday Night FEVER

7 Type of shoes: PLATFORM

12 Big APPLE (where disco began)

14 Disco queen: DONNA (Sommer)

15 Plant: FERN

Check out more fun and games at
www.GrandparentsRock.com

Upcoming Books in the

Grandparents ROCK™ Series

GRANDPARENTS ROCK
The
MONEY
and Grandparenting Guide
for the Rock-n-Roll Generation

A prosperous generation that believes in living life to its fullest, Boomers spend, save, earn and invest money in unique ways—especially in relation to their grandkids. Discover how members of the Rock-n-Roll Generation use money to enhance their relationships with their grandkids, how grandparents who expected to outlive their retirement savings and find there's not enough are generating revenue without leaving home ... and how they teach their hard-won financial lessons to their grandkids.

GRANDPARENTS ROCK
The
BUSY BOOMERS
Grandparenting Guide
for the Rock-n-Roll Generation

Boomers are busier than ever, because they're working longer and living a more active lifestyle than previous generations. Enjoy stories and valuable wisdom from Boomers who juggle their work, hobbies, and social lives … while maintaining an active role in their grandkids' life.

GRANDPARENTS ROCK
The
SPIRITUALITY
and Grandparenting Guide
for the Rock-n-Roll Generation

Welcoming a grandchild into the world often opens a new door spiritually for grandparents. This uplifting book will share heart-warming stories about the journeys Boomers have experienced while exploring their own spirituality, what role spirituality and religion has played in their development into grandparents, and how they're are passing on spiritual lessons and beliefs to their grandchildren.

GRANDPARENTS ROCK
The
DATING
and Grandparenting Guide
for the Rock-n-Roll Generation

First they shattered the taboo of divorce. Now many rock-n-roll grandparents find themselves in the ironic and sometimes-awkward position of venturing into the dating pool alongside their grandkids. In this frank and charming book, you'll find insightful and often humorous stories about how single Boomer grandparents handle the challenges of dating, how they balance the conflicting roles of nurturing grandparent and hot date, and how they incorporated their new partners into their extended family.

GRANDPARENTS ROCK
The
ROCKERS
Grandparenting Guide
for the Rock-n-Roll Generation

You were their fan in the 1960's. Now hear how your favorite rock-n-roll stars are handling the transition from music idols to hard-rockin' grandparents. Discover how music has influenced their roles as grandparents ... how they use music to bond with their grandkids ... and what messages they're sending to their fellow Boomer grandparents via their music and lyrics.

ABOUT THE AUTHOR

Pat Burns is passionate about inspiring people to live life to the fullest, a mission she lives daily as a popular speaker, enlightened entrepreneur and, of course, hands-on grandmother.

As President of Mark Victor Hansen's Mega Inner Circle, Inc., Pat teaches enlightened millionaires around the world ways to positively impact the planet and humanity. On a local level, Pat lives her dream of being a literary philanthropist by serving as Cofounder and Executive Director of the nonprofit 501(c)(3) company Timeless Learning Inc., which produces the Orange County Children's Book Festival (www.kidsbookfestival.com). Her devotion to inspiring the joy of reading draws just under 20,000 people to this annual Southern California family book festival.

In true Boomer fashion, Pat is a trailblazer in the business world, serving as a superstar salesperson, international consultant, and marketing guru for major corporations, state governmental agencies and national associations.

Pat's two grown daughters, whom she raised for many years as a single mother, live in Scottsdale, Arizona, and Vail, Colorado. A resident of Southern California, Pat is the VERY proud grandmother of Dylan and Skye, the cutest kids on the entire planet.